Evolution
of a Student

LISA D. HOPKINS

DEDICATION

For my Mom, who has always been my favorite teacher: Thank you from the bottom of my heart for all you have helped me to understand about life and how to live it. Your unconditional love, compassion and patience are unparalleled. I love you. (PS Thank you also for creating the book's cover. I knew you could do it!)

CONTENTS

CONTENTS

ACKNOWLEDGEMENTS

For every teacher who has dared to educate me: my gratitude for putting up with me while I learned.

For Third Avenue, Nettie Hartnett, East Junior High, Leavenworth High School, Kansas State University, Donnelly College and Cleveland Chiropractic College: I am one of the countless students who have passed through your doors with a quest to dream bigger and become a more authentic expression of myself. My thanks.

For my fellow students and peers: Your support and passion for learning have inspired my own.

A special thank you to my editor, Jennifer Flaspohler. You are a beautiful Light in the world who has made the book writing experience a sincere joy. I love you, Jen.

A very loving thank you to my friend Trace Shapiro. Your support, encouragement and inspiration have been invaluable to me. I love you, T.

PREFACE

All I saw coming toward me was a freshly licked thumb. I was defenseless against the horrific act to come. My friend Andy, with a concerned look rippling across his face, launched his opposable digit squarely against my cheek and rubbed with vigor. Satisfied, he removed his offending weapon. Only when our eyes met and he could see the terror on my face did he absorb the extent of his unwelcome advance. The corners of his eyelids crinkled like foiled chewing gum wrappers and squirted a faint drip of tears. He was actually laughing.

"Ewwwwwwww!" I screamed, half-laughing myself. "I haven't been licked like that since my mom spit shined me for grade school. Gross. I can't believe you licked me!"

Andy laughed so hard, I saw his stomach contort beneath his tightly stretched t-shirt.

"I just saw a smudge and..." he gasped, "I couldn't help myself."

After a heavy dowsing of soap and water, we laughed and walked out the door to enjoy our movie night. It's funny how

1

little events can dredge up past memories from the neural network of your brain. I had childhood flashbacks for months of my mom slathering spittle on me and then rushing me out the door for school. Who could concentrate on learning anything with the delightfully distracting scent of hours old coffee and toothpaste plastered to your skin? And sealing it with a kiss didn't make me feel any better.

My mom was such a decent, hard working woman that I initially intended to forgive this small offense; however, sending me to that cold institution of learning on top of it all was reprehensible. Once the two events were linked in my mind, spittle and kindergarten, I found neither offering a forgivable offense.

MRS. LEARY

I don't remember much of my first year of school. I don't even remember my first day. What I do remember is being stripped from my daily routine with my Grandma Hopkins, or Nanny as we called her, and thrust into a dank brick building with other obnoxious mutants that were roughly my height.

No more waking to breakfast at my own leisurely pace. No more watching my grandma's "programs" with her in the afternoons. Nanny would have to watch Young, Restless people all alone and Search for Tomorrows with someone else's Guiding Light. I would not be there to protect her from the vampires that came for her during the Dark Shadows of late afternoon. If I was lucky, I'd be home in time to help her Court Eddie's Father. We'd still snuggle up in front of the tv on Incredible Hulk night. And she would explain once again why Eddie's Father was a decent dad during the day, but underwent a metamorphosis and turned into a green monster of raging justice by night. I didn't understand the concept of actors playing different roles at that age. What I knew was that Nanny loved the Hulk as much as I did. I knew Nanny loved play time outdoors in the sunshine and pushing me on swing sets. I felt sorry for her, really. She would me missing me.

How could she continue to develop her coloring book art skills without me helping her practice? And I'm pretty sure those grilled cheese and grape jelly sandwiches she always made were not going to eat themselves. Still, I noted a look of relief on her face every morning that I shuffled off to school.

When I arrived at Third Avenue Elementary School, I was reticent to open up and be part of a group. I was a loner by nature. I didn't understand these children and I wasn't sure I really wanted to do so. I couldn't grasp why the little girl with the matted hair splattered glue onto her fingers, blew on it, picked it, rolled it up and then ate it. And what of the booger eating genius sitting a few desks away. The girl who sat in front of me was most disturbing. She smelled like raw sewage and that's not exactly a friendship starter. I was casually fascinated by the clean, rather normal kids who stared at our teacher with such adoration and disciplined attentiveness. I wasn't fascinated enough to strike up a friendship, however. In fact, I wasn't even really there. My body showed up, but my mind was a million miles away.

Our teacher introduced herself as Mrs. Leary and gave us a brief tour of our sparse accommodations. She led us in a single file line to the closet we'd be placing our coats and umbrellas in. I was half paying attention. The only thing I noticed was that Mrs. Leary was cute. Had she not been such an intriguing human study, I'd have flung myself out of one of the half-opened windows and ran home to my freedom.

I listened to Mrs. Leary as much as I could stand every day and then I'd drift into my own world. I'd take stock of her natural blond hair which was cropped short; spiky on the top and sides and longer in back. She looked like Rod Stewart, though it was unlikely that with her dowdy outfits we'd ever see her show up in tight leather pants and sing a rendition of "Hot Legs."

Every day, Mrs. Leary would instruct us through lessons that I was simultaneously bored and confused by. I'd sit, slumped in my chair, waiting for personal instruction. When she'd finally make her way to my desk and her starry blue eyes locked in on mine, I knew she was expressing concern for me in her own way. *How is it that you can be so smug about kindergarten?* she seemed to wonder.

Finally, she would take us outside into the open emporium of play. Swing sets, jungle gyms, basketball hoops, a chalked outline of hopscotch and a metal backdrop to catch softballs and kickballs were all separated by a wide open space filled in with chalky gravel. At last, I found an area I excelled in. Recess. I hit the doors leading outside every day with enthusiasm, but once beyond the structured classroom, I didn't know what to do first. I'd try to touch base with every inch of the playground experience. I'd play for awhile, but then sadly realize that on the playground I felt most alone. It is the one place I didn't want to be alone.

Some mean kids would taunt me and a few others with fat jokes. The others cried or slunk away. I stood my ground and bested them. I force fed their humiliation right back to them. I had a big brother whose foul language far surpassed five year olds with a few fat jokes. I opened up an arsenal of insults that shut them down fast.

I wasn't completely untouched by their words. I knew I wasn't fat, but I had started to realize that I was carrying a little extra weight than others. I noticed the frail, underfed children around me and thought, they must not have a Nanny who feeds them. I considered myself fortunate. Still, I wanted to blend in and that wasn't going to happen if I didn't morph into a sizable replication of my peers. My ultimate decision to fit in was to rush everyone on the playground and insist on playing whatever was available to play. I would fit in everywhere. At first, it was a great plan, but quickly became exhausting. A lot of girls couldn't relate to my tomboy nature. A few timid boys were already afraid of strong women. The weird kids, I avoided. The rest were like me, gently seeking acceptance somewhere. I eventually found that the popular boys liked me a lot because I could play football and thus they became my people. I was indoctrinated into the pool of the chosen kids.

One day, I was asked to join an elite group. It was an organization founded by a young boy who always announced his name in three chunks: first name, middle and last. "I'm Christopher Gunther Anderson." He would announce it like he was a super hero. I never used my full name so I simply said, "I'm Lisa." We had made fast friends during football games, but the newly forming secret society would challenge our goodwill.

"I'll join," I told him solidly, "but only if I'm the President."

"But you can't be President."

I could feel heat in my face. "And why not?" I demanded.

"Because…" he laughed into my humiliation, "you're a girl."

"Oh yeah?"

And that's when it hit him. My fist.

The rest of recess went blurry. I know Mrs. Leary sprinted towards us and separated us. Chris was sobbing and I was simply standing before Mrs. Leary waiting to be punished. I'm pretty sure I was placed on the wall of shame, which simply meant that I had to go stand against the back wall of the institution. We were not allowed to interact with anyone while we stood there, holding up the crumbling bricks with our backs. Occasionally someone tried to find out what were in for, but were quickly summoned away unless they "wanted to join us."

It was a special surprise to my mom, being called in for a parent-teacher conference so early in my academic career. My brother, a master at causing mischief, hadn't even started rebelling in school until junior high. My parents had already lowered the bar of expectations with him, but somehow Mom didn't suspect it would have to be lowered to less than 3 feet to accommodate me.

Mom was weary when she had to rearrange her work day to meet with Mrs. Leary. I'm sure she was thinking, *Oh no, not this crap again.* Well, she would've thought it, if Mom actually used that language.

When Mom arrived home, she didn't look upset. She sat down with me on my bed and more gently than I expected said, "I talked to your teacher today."

I nodded. I didn't trust where this was going at all. I kept my lips tight and a protective scowl on my face.

"She said that you hit a young boy in your class."

I nodded and then I defended. "He told me I couldn't be president of his group because I was a girl." I was fighting for justice in my mind, defending equal rights for women or something like that.

"You know that you should never hit anyone. It is not the way to solve problems."

I stared at her blankly. Mom had never hit anyone in her life. I knew that. The same could not be said of my dad.

"Mrs. Leary said that the little boy was crying and that you just stood there. Mrs. Leary is concerned because you didn't apologize and you didn't cry."

I looked at my sweet mom as sincerely as I could and answered the unasked question. "Why would I cry? I wasn't the one who got hit?"

I thought my mom would break into a million tiny tears. I never touched another person in any harmful way again.

MISS BUSEY

The only evidence I had that I'd passed kindergarten was a card that boasted a series of S +'s and time off for good behavior. I would learn that the S+'s stood for Satisfactory + and the time off was called summer vacation. Delusional from my reestablishment of a routine with my Nanny again, I felt betrayed three months later when my mom came at me with a thumb full of saliva and a song in her heart, "School Days." What fresh hell could this mean?

I was once again hustled awake at an obscene hour and delivered to the doorsteps of the institution. Don't you love me? I wanted to cry. Instead, I sucked it up and turned away from the relieved looks of my family.

Once inside the doors, I was instructed to a homeroom class led by a militant black lady named Miss Busey. She adjusted her wire rimmed glasses and toyed with a tightly spun bun riding the back of her head before commanding us to stand at attention. She placed her hand over her heart and told us to do the same. We faced a flag and she demanded we repeat after her. What tumbled out of her mouth was some allegiance to the flag. None of us understood a word. She had us remain standing as she sat down at the front of the class on a piano bench. She started banging on warped keys that were so out of tune that whatever song she was going for was lost on our first grade class.

I knew what an organ sounded like. My maternal grandparents had one at their house. Their organ looked like Miss Busey's contraption, but it didn't sound like it at all. I was never inclined to protect my ears when anyone played the organ, except when someone pushed the piano feature on the organ's key pad and stale memories of Miss Busey shell shocked my eardrums. I'd dive behind anything creating a sound barrier to get away. Yet even the piano feature of the organ sounded better than Miss Busey's honky tonk noise maker.

To further the assault, Miss Busey would sing along and accompany herself, encouraging us to do the same. I only knew a few songs at the time and she sang none of them. I'd do my best to sing along to the proposed ditties she chose, but I couldn't say that I knew what I was singing about. The songs I knew were the ones Nanny taught me to sing before bed. After leading me in the spoken version of the Lord's Prayer, we'd sing one song about a drunk monkey who went to an animal fair and another about Old Joe Fagan. He had a pig that died. Joe and his wife committed suicide in their grief. Yeah, I didn't know what I was singing then, either.

I got the better end of Nanny's song selections. My sister had to sing about two little girls in blue whose Mom died. My brother is the only one who made it out of those nightly rituals unscathed. He doesn't remember them.

I sat in Miss Busey's class thinking she was a dictator. She rarely smiled or laughed. People in town called her an old maid. I never understood that notion. Why would she clean houses when she had a perfectly good job as a teacher? Times must have been tough.

Miss Busey and I didn't see eye to eye and it wasn't at all because of my height. I enjoyed creative freedom. She liked rules. I'm sure that it was out of her sheer lack of imagination that she forced us to learn the state birds of all 50 states. To do so, she handed out traced drawings of birds and demanded that we color them in with their distinctive, appropriate colors. Not only did I dislike being restricted in my color palette, I also hated having to color within the lines of those copied photos. I chose colors I liked, instead. And she reprimanded me. I paid little attention to the lines. And she made a pass once a day by my desk to check my work. One day she stared at my Picasso-like project before her eyes. I was beaming with pride at my work.

"You did not stay within the lines. You will stay in for your full recess and color this correctly." With that, she handed me a blank outline of a bloated bird.

I sat inside the entire recess and picked at a scab I'd assembled from navigating my seatless bicycle. One jagged channel of cracked dirt on our backyard hill pitched my bike so successfully that I soared over the handle bars and skidded across the earth on my elbows. The delicate pieces of rock and glass hibernating in our grass tore at my tender skin mercilessly. The entire half hour I picked meticulously and refused to color, in defiance. I'd earned that scab and I intended to pick its cracked goodness until it oozed. Miss Busey came back in with my class, saw my blood and didn't react at all.

"Your bird's not done," she said dispassionately.

Eventually she overpowered me. I colored within her parameters, even though inside I was rebelling at the injustice.

Once I was old enough, I realized I just simply couldn't think of this woman fondly. If I saw her today, I'd probably trace a figure all my own. "Hey, Miss Busey, here. I've got a bird for you. Be sure to color it in flesh tones and read between the lines."

MRS. VAKAS

No one ever tells you that education can come with a hidden cost. Your family, by nature of your last name, leaves a daunting legacy for you to follow. I was blessed to attend a different elementary school than my siblings. My parents had moved and I was barely out of the geographical cut off range to attend their schools.

My older sister, Debbie, was a trailblazer of good behavior and pioneered her way through school with quiet servitude and good grades. My older brother, Mark, couldn't care less. He was a charming trouble maker who had potential, but squandered it on disobedience. He was just as smart as my sister, but as my mom repeated, "He just didn't apply himself." I had no idea what that meant, but I knew what their legacy meant for me, either open arm embracement or the shutter-blind-rolling-eyelids that indicated disappointment from my teachers. All I shared of either of them was DNA and a last name, but somehow teachers know which families their students come from and judge accordingly.

Lucky for me, Mrs. Vakas was a transplant from my siblings's school, but she had Debbie as her pupil. She transferred before Mark found his way into her class. Debbie had won Mrs. Vakas's heart and by default, I did, too. Debbie had smoothly paved the way for me to coast into the arms of the friendliest teacher I'd had so far.

My very first day in her class, she beamed at me, "Are you Debbie's sister?"

I hesitated. My answer truly depended on whether she'd had a favorable experience with my sister or not.

"Yes?" I answered in the form of a question.

"Well, she's something very special. I adored your sister. I'm so happy to have you in my class."

Whew.

Mrs. Vakas was a large Greek woman with big bones. I think that's what I heard my family say. She had salt and pepper hair and a twinkle in her eyes that let every child know they were safe and important. She encouraged us and made us feel that we could do anything. When she got up from her desk to write on the chalkboard or wander nearby to check on our work, I noticed that she distributed her weight unevenly to her favored side. Her waddling gait reminded me of my Nanny. I felt further at ease.

I loved second grade. I worked hard for Mrs. Vakas and really tried to understand the lessons. As an added perk, Mrs. Vakas allowed another young boy in my class and me to share our homemade books. What started out as gentle sharing became a race to see who could create the most stories. Every night I indulged myself in a pastime I already enjoyed. I wrote and drew stick figures and told stories. Every day I'd leap up and get ready for school, waiting for the hour when I could present them to the class.

The other author, Sean, used to taunt me and try to establish his dominion over the book writing experience. He showed other children his art work and exaggerated what he assumed was superior skill. I knew another boy named Travis drew better than he did, but Travis never wrote stories to share. Someone had to challenge this intellectual bully, so I did. It was less about competition for me initially and more about languishing in my hobby. For Sean, it was a cutthroat game of sheer numbers. With that intent in play, I made it a point to write one or two books a night. He'd feverishly compete with me and we'd show up the following day ready to share. Our classmates loved it. They couldn't tell the difference between a professionally written book or our creative masterpieces. They didn't care. It was pure entertainment for them. Mrs. Vakas would listen attentively and try not to let on how amused she found herself over our competitive spirit. She encouraged us all the more.

We'd sit together in class, Sean and I, he writing with his left hand and I with my right. Elbow to elbow we'd scribble out our latest best sellers. Sean is what I learned was called a south paw. It forced him to have to hook his arm and wrap it in a semicircle to write on our average sized, right hand biased desks. He was an anomaly in our classroom. I understood my brother suffered the same affliction. No one tied them up and forced them to write with the other hand, which throughout history had been cruelly attempted. It really didn't bother me much, though sometimes at dinner when Mark and I would bump elbows trying to eat, I admit that a rope might have saved me a lot of missed spoonfuls. A noose would've saved even more. Admittedly, I found their unique feature quite fascinating, but not fascinating enough to give up my right-handed, privileged advantage.

Sean and I wrote increasingly more books every day. Sean from his left-handed view of the world, me from my right. At the end of the year, I'd amassed 200 short stories. Sean had long ago given up the fight.

"I lost interest," he posited with snobbish deflection.

"You got beat," I snapped back.

Our daily trash talk only lasted until we reached the outside doors for recess. I don't know why he let me do it day in and out, but I would find him high up on a jungle gym and stand below him. With careful delicacy, I'd untie his shoelaces and lash them around the metal rods of the geodesic dome upon which he sat. Once I tied his laces twenty or thirty knots deep, inevitably the bell would toll and I'd run away and leave him stranded by his sneakers, yelling for help, atop the jungle gym. If he ever ratted me out, I wouldn't know. None of my teachers ever said anything. They probably figured, "If you're dumb enough to let her do it, you deserve it."

I'm pretty sure, though, that Mrs. Vakas knew. She just loved Debbie enough to overlook it. Deep down, with her mirth of spirit, she probably secretly enjoyed that I'd lassoed the pain in the ass in the first place. It was one less kid to keep track of.

Toward the end of the year, an older man that I recognized from my grandparents' church, showed up. He took each student one by one from our classroom and led us to the scarcely used auditorium. When it was my turn, he walked me onto an empty stage, handed me a plastic fluted toy and asked me to blow into it.

"This is a kazoo," he explained. "Next year, you will be taking a band class. You will have to pick an instrument beforehand. This will help you choose."

I yet don't know the logic behind blowing into the nasally sounding, spit laden tube that amplified your own humming. It didn't help me pick an instrument because no one plays anything that sounds like a honking goose. Truthfully, it sounded a lot like Miss Busey's piano. There was no way in hell I was playing that, either. This kind old fellow asked me if I knew what instrument I'd like to play. Without hesitation, I chose the path my sister had already left behind for me. "The saxophone," I said resolutely.

"The saxophone, eh?" He smiled. "Well, that's a mighty fine instrument."

"My sister played one," I proudly admitted.

"Oh?" His ears pricked up. "And who is your sister?"

"Debbie."

"Ahhh… Debbie. I had her as a pupil. She was quite good at the saxophone."

I smiled. Band class? Coast cleared. Thanks, Debbie!

REIMANN, BLUME & FRAGNER, OH MY!

Third grade was a challenging year for me. Third Avenue Elementary was K-2, so all of my classmates and I would be entering the big kids school, Nettie Hartnett. It was named after some prominent older lady in our community. For the next four years, I was stuck in a new building and truthfully, I kind of looked forward to it. That is until I met my third grade homeroom teacher.

Ms. Reimann was a strict, ginger haired teacher with freckles. She reminded me of a friend of my sister who also favored the red hued hair and had a smattering of freckles. As an adult, we tend to consider that all types of people are beautiful. Most kids are freaked out by freckles and I was not excluded from this group. I would stare. I couldn't figure out what had happened to her that she looked like an Easter egg every day. I examined my own skin and couldn't find any evidence that hers was normal. Asian people, black people and white people I understood, of course. But freckled people made me pause. They were alien to me. Ms. Reimann also wore her Rapunzel hair to her ankles. It startled my senses.

I was disappointed with my homeroom. I had quickly figured

out that all of my friends were in another teacher's homeroom. Ms. Blume. I liked her a lot and longed to be in her class. I hadn't had her for a teacher, but she was beautiful in my eyes. She had dark hair and brown eyes and reminded me of a kiss of chocolate. I had my first crush on a teacher, though I didn't know it at the time.

Ms. Reimann was a disciplinarian much like Miss Busey. She didn't put up with foolishness or so she threatened. The truth is she put up with a lot from a sandy haired nuisance named Jay. He was a transfer student. Read: Another school had willed him to ours in hopes we could shapeshift his incorrigible ways. Ms. Reimann quickly tethered herself to my hate list when she sat the disruptive boob next to me. Every day he tried to talk to me, getting us both in trouble. He was also an incredible bully. He would hit other children on the playground and torment them in classrooms. He picked on me every day. I couldn't stand him. Yet, I had no desire to fight him. I'd outgrown that in kindergarten.

Couple my deep desire to be away from him with the overwhelming depression that my Nanny had passed away just a few months into the new school year and I was spiraling down a rabbit hole that even my parents noticed.

When asked what was wrong, I told my mom the story of Jay. I wasn't going to because I always tried to tough out situations, but I was miserable. I relented and let her in. She told my dad and the events that ensued were awe inspiring.

"I'm going in to school with you today," my dad informed me as we hopped into my brother's newly restored Camaro.

"OK." I was stricken inside with fear. Mom usually handled all of the school conferences and matters of academics. She was polite and kind. My dad had a side that spread fear at home and I couldn't imagine toting that reputation into public view.

He was mad, I could tell. I thought I was in trouble. He assured me that he simply wanted to talk with my teacher.

When we walked in together, I was a slumped ball of nerves, hiding behind him. He told me to take my seat and I did so obediently.

I could see that Ms. Reimann and my dad were engaged in a death match at the front of the classroom. She insisted something. He insisted another. At one point, our whole class turned around to listen in on the commotion. I could've pickled in humiliation.

"Is that your dad?" a sweet girl next to me asked.

"Yes," I cowered.

The bell rang and they continued to argue. I fell into an ashen pile in my seat.

"I don't want her anywhere near that boy." My dad pointed to Jay, the little punk who was now quivering in his seat.

"I put Lisa there because she is a good student and I think she's a good influence on Jay," Ms. Reimann defended her actions. She gave me a half-smile and then glared at Jay.

Jay cowered at this point. The whole class was glowering at him. He brought this wrath upon our homeroom class and they were finally fed up. They stared at me, only because it was my parent who stood up and battled for our justice. If they only knew, my dad was really battling just for me.

"I want her removed from your class this instant. I will not let her stay here."

When Ms. Reimann protested and tried to reason, she suddenly looked like we did under her flaring temper. Scared.

Ms. Reimann refused his request and my dad tore into her with language I'd only heard at home. The foul language he used superseded my own comprehension of the words and suddenly I saw him, eyes popped open with rage, motioning me to get my books and follow him. I did as I was told.

"All of the homerooms are full, Mr. Hopkins. Where do you think she's going to go?"

"They're probably full for a reason. No one wants to be in your class. She's going to Ms. Blume's class. End of story."

I kind of smirked at that one. Praise the Lord, I was going to Ms. Blume's class.

By the time the second bell rang that morning, I had already taken up residence in my new classroom. Familiar, surprised faces glistened with joy. My best friends welcomed me in with ecstatic waves, motioning me to sit by them. I had to be simply exhausted from my travels one door down and they wanted me to rest that instant. Ms. Blume had other ideas. She put me on the far side of the room from the welcome committee between two students I knew, but was not especially close. She was more austere than I remembered. Apparently her understanding of the morning's events had been tainted by Ms. Reimann. For only Ms. Reimann had the disposition to poison the well of Ms. Blume's ordinarily good spirits.

Ms. Blume handled me sternly that day. She was challenged to find room for me in her packed classroom, but she made do. By the day's end, I had settled in quite nicely. Cozy, even.

Ms. Blume. Ahhh, I loved her. I don't know what it was about her, either. Perhaps it was the way she wore those vests with matching slacks which always gave her the appearance of perpetually performing in some high school chorale concert. Short sleeves and long sleeves were interchangeable, but she'd be damned if she'd change her signature look. She was probably mid-30's and had the unique ability to sound both soft spoken and commanding at the same time. I listened. I worked at school, but just enough to get by. I missed Nanny. It was starting to show in my slacking motivation.

After I received a B on a test, Ms. Blume asked to see me after school. A "B" wasn't all that bad and I was prepared to shrug it off when I was capsized by Ms. Blume's warpath sneak attack.

"Lisa, you are working well below your level. You're smarter than this. I know you are and you are not trying very hard."

I was shocked. How could she know that? Truth is, she could

see it written all over my bored and distressed face. I was depressed, but I was also pulling good grades without trying. She knew I wasn't applying myself at all.

"Mrs. Escher is having an after school meeting for students wishing to enter an accelerated program. I want you in that class. I think it's in your best interest. It would mean staying after school an extra hour every day with the rest of the students, but all of you will then enter an advanced placement curriculum and take classes one grade above the level you're working now. Does someone pick you up after school?"

I was still numb from being busted so successfully. "No. I walk home."

"Good, then you can let your parents know what I plan for you and see what arrangements can be made."

Even though this advanced curriculum sounded like a choice, I didn't feel like I really had one. Ms. Blume wanted me in that class. I wasn't going to disappoint her. Plus I was bored with the current topics of interest. Mostly, though, I felt like someone finally noticed and believed in me. That mattered most. No one had ever said I was intelligent before, even though my grades usually reflected it. Ms. Blume gave me the opportunity of a lifetime and I felt it even then. I was scared, though.

"Don't worry. Mrs. Escher is a good teacher and she'll have you primed in no time for the advanced work."

Mrs. Escher was the other third grade teacher. She was scary.

I didn't know how I'd handle her. She was a no-nonsense lady who wore blazers every day. To this day, I remember the canary yellow one. It must've been a personal favorite for her. She also wore these obnoxiously colored necklaces made out of bulbous beads strung together. They looked like the deep end divider buoys at the local swimming pool.

Ms. Blume was right, though. I was considerably more enthusiastic about my studies once I started hanging out with Mrs. Escher for that one hour after school. I liked her, gruff as she was, and I suspected beneath her no bs approach, that she liked me.

Ms. Blume will go down in my log books as the teacher that most changed my life. She gave me hope. When I was 8, had just lost my grandmother and felt disconnected from the world around me, that mattered to me.

I still have a poloroid of her waving to me at a Christmas concert, wearing what else? A plaid vest and matching pants.

I entered the fourth grade as an advanced student thanks to Ms. Blume. My new teacher, Mrs. Fragner, nearly kissed me for being such an academic angel in her class. She lavished her loving attention on me immediately and made me her pet. I adored her. She was a mom and it showed in how she related to us. She was about my own mom's age and a military wife, I was sure of it. We lived in a military town and one year she just appeared. I didn't recognize her. She wasn't a staple in our small town so she must have been a transplant from some exotic section of our country, like Fort Bragg. I'd heard about that place a lot. We didn't have a lot of military kids in our classes until junior high. They did their K-6 on Fort Leavenworth's base and then many of them descended upon the locals via our school system. I rather liked it both ways. The comfortable familiarity of my hometown families and the desegregated mixing of military families with us.

Mrs. Fragner was incredibly kind and a fantastic teacher. When another equally wonderful teacher lost her daughter to words like "rape" and "murder", Mrs. Fragner coddled us on low speed until we could comprehend that our other teacher was struggling just to get by. I always appreciated that she cared to check in with how we were doing. She was a rock in a storm.

At the close of fourth grade, she handed me a picture of herself with a sentimental note written on back. Every now and then I rediscover that photo and find those hazel eyes staring at me with the biggest smile, her black hair cut like a modified bee hive with two little handlebars hanging down near her ears. It takes me right back. I enjoyed Mrs. Fragner, but more importantly I enjoyed being a real student in her class. I had made straight A's every year, but it meant more that year because I'd finally been challenged enough to earn them.

MRS. LAUXMAN

When you meet your "people" you know. Debbie Lauxman, my fifth grade teacher, was my people. She wasn't syrupy or saccharine in disposition, she was a fabulous blend somewhere in the middle of the scale. She wasn't exactly transparent in her affection for her students, but you could tell in rare moments that she cared deeply.

I was smitten with Mrs. Lauxman right off. I talked my mom's ears off about my allegiance.

"Did I tell you what Mrs. Lauxman did today?" "Said today?" "Wore today?" The segues were always different, but the outcome was the same. A twenty or thirty minute conversation about my favorite topic. More, if my mom would let me.

My mom was polite at first, but after the twentieth Mrs. Lauxman story of the night, every day, for months, my mom snapped in her own gentle way. "You sure do like Mrs. Lauxman, don't you?" That's as harsh as Mom gets.

Mom's words, much to her disappointment, only encouraged me. "Oh yes, she's my favorite. Did I tell you about...?"

My mom would finish washing her dishes, quietly wishing she could snap them apart with her mind. Sometimes she'd just bag the whole idea and walk away, hoping to distract me. I'd follow her. She'd begin tasks that she knew I'd hate and I'd join her, still lauding praises over Mrs. Debbie Lauxman. My mom would try to leave without me, but I'd beat her to the car. My poor mom didn't realize that she would always be my absolute favorite, but she'd have to earn it. Her part of that exchange was listening to tales about my favorite teacher.

Mrs. Lauxman was hipper than most teachers. She understood us and what was important to us. She spoke our language. We wished we could speak hers. We picked up a hint of an accent and through a thorough questionnaire I designed, our class found out that she was from some magical land called St. Louis. It was 5 hours from us, but could've been a whole country away for all we knew.

Mrs. Lauxman was so gracious when she accepted the questionnaire to fill out. Her smile seemed inextricably linked to the excited glimmer in her eyes. The wider her smile, the more her eyes danced inside me with a connection that gave me a visceral reaction in my heart space. I loved Mrs. Lauxman. I was infatuated with her and everything about her titillated me.

I carried that questionnaire everywhere. It wore itself into a tattered bit of vaguely lined pulp after awhile, but I wouldn't relinquish it for anything.

I learned from her responses that her birthday was in December, right before my January birthday, so we were soul mates of sorts. I knew that her husband Larry taught art at a local college and they had a son. (Another baby would be added later). Her favorite color was black. She loved tennis. And she worshipped the Rolling Stones.

It was inevitable that I would start wearing black and consider it my favorite color, until my art teacher a few years later told me it was considered a "neutral."

I took up tennis and became quite skilled at it. I wound up having a love affair with the sport and was the number one seed for my high school jv team in singles and then in doubles my senior year. I was offered a full ride scholarship to play tennis at a small college in Kansas, but I turned it down to go to a larger university. I didn't realize until after I graduated that I could've walked on if I'd tried.

I also instantly revered the Rolling Stones.

"Hey Mom, can I get this album?" I inquired while we wandered around Wal-Mart.

"What is it?"

"The Rolling Stones."

My mom puzzled over the selection. Up until then, my music was directed toward catchy pop tunes and long drawn out comic book readings of the Incredible Hulk on 45's. Mom knew my musical tastes intimately because every Sunday since my Nanny passed away, we'd escape to my brother's room, where the hi-fi was stored, and play music together. Sunday was always a turbulent day in our household. With all of the arguments my dad would instigate, Mom and I would ultimately find our way to the sanctity of Mark's old bedroom and take turns playing our music for one another. We'd dance and sing our hearts out and find peace of mind. That tradition was fading, however. I was playing sports a lot so there was no time. Instead, I'd broadcast my music from my bedroom so the entire household could enjoy it. It was no doubt the first thing on Mom's mind when she saw the album cover and wondered what the contents beyond the cellophane wrapper would do to her eardrums. It's not like I didn't appreciate different kinds of music, Mark had introduced me to a lot. I had the album *Back in Black* long before Mrs. Lauxman entered the picture. Maybe Mom's consideration of that nightmare made her relent.

"Oh, okay. Put it in the cart."

"Really?" I was beside myself with joy.

Mom was far too distracted with her shopping experience and greeting people she knew to question why I'd chosen the album. We were driving home when she finally asked me, "So what made you want this album?"

"Well, it's Mrs. Lauxman's favorite. You see…"

I think my mom wanted to careen the car into a telephone pole.

**

30

Evolution of a Student

In Mrs. Lauxman's fifth grade class, we enjoyed silent reading hour. It was the first year for it. I think that someone in administration decided that break times should be extended and thus silent reading hour was proposed and put to a vote. Anxious teachers' hands likely shot straight up. "Pick ME!" Emphatic "yes" votes put the built in snooze fest into place.

I rather enjoyed silent reading hour. I picked extremely complicated novels and brought them in to woo Mrs. Lauxman into seeing my progressive attitude toward education. I couldn't quite get into her favorite author, Kurt Vonnegut, at that age, but I made up for it with Peter Benchley's *Jaws*. I had nightmares for weeks. I should have known better. The movie terrified me. I don't know what made me think the book would be any better. Still, we were never instructed on what reading was appropriate. Any reading that entertained us into quietude would do.

Later in our school year, Mrs. Lauxman allowed us to bring in music to share. I understood the value in this and readily summoned my focus to pore through hours of songs for just the right one. Each afternoon, she'd pause to allow a few students to share their selections. I don't remember mine so much as that of the new little trouble maker in our grade who brought in his copy of "I Love Rock N' Roll." With Joan Jett as his back-up, he sang and danced on his desktop. Mrs. Lauxman permitted it and was thoroughly entertained. Music, the mouthpiece of barely expressed emotions. Our class allowed ourselves to be heard in those moments and our teacher was listening.

Oh and how much she was listening.

The same trouble maker and I found ourselves in a compromised situation one afternoon near our lockers. Everyone had cleared out and we were the stragglers left behind, haggling over a decision we'd mutually made. He had stolen a cigarette from a family member at home. He wanted to try it. I had been his partner in crime for the planning, but when it came down to it, I was less interested in the exploration of a nasty habit. I was interested to see what Mrs. Lauxman would do. Did she really care about us? More specifically, did she really care about me? I was struggling at home knowing the difference between being loved and truly cared about and being used as a pawn in the adult world of, "Look what you're doing to the kids." That was my cue to stand in the kitchen with a pitiful look on my face and demonstrate the effects that parental poor choices were having upon me. I was playing a selfish trust game at school that day and I didn't consider the position I put that poor trouble making peer of mine in. My deeper intentions were innocent enough, but I felt bad later.

Mrs. Lauxman walked out of her classroom when I said, deliberately loud, "Give it to me."

The troubled student responded in a faint whisper, "Not until we get outside."

Mrs. Lauxman rushed us full steam and demanded to know what we were up to. She saw the cigarette peeking from the boy's hand and ushered us into her classroom. She closed the door. I knew she couldn't believe that I was a part of it, being such an exemplary student and all. Shamefully, I was equally as responsible as the other kid.

After asking the obvious questions which forced us to identify the offending object and admit to its natural owner, Mrs. Lauxman hauled it into custody. She sternly expressed disappointment, but I could see compassion in her eyes. She didn't want to reprimand us, but felt obliged to follow through.

"I'm not going to tell your parents, but I never want to see you doing this again." She took a moment to find the appropriate words, "Never take up a habit that you cannot afford to keep." That sentence landed squarely into my brain to be stored for years to come.

My peer stood there motionless, not taking any of it in. I stood there admiring my teacher, who now saw a bad side in me that really didn't exist, and handling us with tenderness and fairness.

"So you care about us?" I finally cut to the chase.

She dramatically came to our sides and placed a hand on both of us, "Of course, I do!" It was in a *how dare you think otherwise* voice.

Satisfied, I walked out the door. The other boy was frustrated, but by the next day we were over it. I had always kept a distance from him and that didn't change, but in class, we spoke and laughed and forgot about the whole thing.

Apparently Mrs. Lauxman did, too. When parent-teacher conferences rolled around, my mom received a glowing report. She came home euphoric. "Mrs. Lauxman sure had a lot of positive things to say about you."

"Really? Like what?" I was all in for this conversation.

Mom plucked out one detail after another and finally said seriously, "She did say that you are more mature than your classmates. She told me that it will take someone older to truly appreciate you."

That line wormed its way into both my mom's mind and my own. I was surrounded by adults, dealt mostly with adult responsibilities and concerns and chose to be a loner, even surrounded by friends. Mrs. Lauxman saw something in me that she likely knew about herself. Born near the same time, we shared a lot of similarities.

At my urging, a few of my classmates and I asked Mrs. Lauxman out on a date. We wanted to take her to a restaurant of her choosing for her birthday. All of us were super excited when she said yes. I was especially excited because she would be coming to my house to pick me up, along with a few other students. We were all bubbling over with anticipation. She was meeting us outside of school and that could only mean one thing, she was our friend.

I spent all day picking out my outfit when the day arrived and bouncing around the house as the clock inched along. My mom was more than ready to push me out the door when I heard the cartoonish beep of Mrs. Lauxman's Toyota. With absent minded adoration and oblivious to the cool factor, I sprinted to her car with a toothy smile that could've grated cheese.

Mrs. Lauxman shifted a few items on her front seat around so I could sit next to her. I was bursting with my good fortune. I couldn't have asked for a better spot. Right next to her.

We had already asked Mrs. Lauxman on our trusty questionnaire what her favorite food was and she told us, Chinese. She could've said a la carte bug guts and we'd have been in favor. Whatever she wanted, we were prepared to dig into our allowances and pay for her meal. We arrived at the restaurant owned by a classmate's parents. Our peer greeted us with menus and was smiling with that same exaggerated grin that the rest of us shared. We must have looked like the *Stepford Wives* to Mrs. Lauxman. How could she know the incredible joy she'd bestowed upon us? We were all writhing in our seats while she looked us over, probably thinking, *I wonder what this Island of Misfit Toys will do with their lives?* Her face told us nothing of the sort, she was lovingly staring at each one of us.

When the menus came, we looked at foreign words longer than our haircuts and wondered where the sandwich section was being hidden. I looked to my peers for support, but they were just as clueless.

Sensing our preoccupation with the menu, Mrs. Lauxman asked, "So who here likes Chinese food?"

All of us squealed excitedly, "I do!" Little frauds, one and all. I don't think a single one of us had ever had a bite of Chinese food, except the restaurant owners' son who was working with his family that night. We had no idea what to order so when he walked by, we whispered our predicament and he rushed to our side. His parents were good sports. They let him take our orders as he diligently explained terms we'd be years from understanding.

I took my cue from Mrs. Lauxman. "I'll have Mu Shu Pork." She gave our young classmate a convincing smile that reassured him we'd all survive somehow and handed him her menu. He came to me next. "That sounds good. I'll have the Mu Shu Pork, too."

I mimicked Mrs. Lauxman's diction and pronunciation in a passable enough way and she gave me an appreciative smile. It wasn't until the food came and I, like my classmates, had to identify what we ordered and how to eat it that the jig was up. Mrs. Lauxman had to be amused, but she was a good teacher. It was a part of her, not something she left at the door every night when she went home. She patiently instructed us on how to eat our menu choices.

I was consternated by the fluid set before me in a decorated gravy boat. I was sure the Chinese had another name for the little pot, but I didn't know it. I stared at the murky, dark fluid within it and wondered about it, but refrained from asking. I didn't want to appear foolish in front of my hero.

"It's plum sauce," Mrs. Lauxman offered.

"Oh. I didn't know."

She poured a little onto her tortilla, I was sure that had another name also, and put the strangled remains of something inside. She drizzled plum sauce on top. Then she nodded to me. I'm pretty sure this monkey see, monkey do demonstration was how the early cave people communicated and I had to say, it was quite effective. I followed her course of actions to the letter and finally landed my hand on the ladle dipped in motor oil. The plum sauce, once I had a taste, was delicious. I had no hesitation in making myself a second helping. I did, however, hesitate to have Chinese food again until high school.

I ended my fifth grade year with tears. Mrs. Lauxman and another teacher, Ms. Grigaitis, rubbed my back as I hung my head dramatically over a bannister near our classroom. I watched my tears drop several stories onto the cement steps below.

"You are going to have a great year next year!" Mrs. Lauxman encouraged.

"Sure, but there won't be you."

"I'm right down the hall," she soothed.

"It's not the same."

"Yes, but you'll have other great teachers." She named them, but I didn't want to move on from her class. There are names for those children who are 18 and still in fifth grade, however. Rejects. I didn't want to be one of those, either.

I left that day, crying the whole walk home.

My mom had a few blissful weeks of not hearing every detail about Mrs. Lauxman. I, on the other hand, was suffering withdrawal. I moped about, listening to the Rolling Stones in wistful memories.

My dad and I had taken up tennis with a serious fervor that

summer which at least aligned me with Mrs. Lauxman somehow. Out of her passion for the sport, grew my own independent interest.

My dad and I played every evening. We watched tennis matches on television, read up on the sport and taught ourselves everything we needed to know. One evening, we ran into Debbie and Larry Lauxman playing tennis. They watched us play and Larry was impressed enough to ask if I'd be willing to meet up and play with them. I was over the moon. I trained that much harder.

One day the phone rang. I picked it up and heard, "Lisa?"

"Yes?" I was already anticipating.

"It's Debbie Lauxman. I was calling to see if you want to go play tennis?"

I put the phone against my chest to muffle the sound and yelled, "Moooooom!!!"

Mom was standing a few feet away drying dishes. "You don't have to yell, I'm right here. What do you need?"

"It's Mrs. Lauxman on the phone..."

I heard my mom sigh and watched her twist her dishtowel into a noose.

MRS. KUPISZEWSKI

I entered the sixth grade without hesitation. My class was finally at the top of the Nettie Hartnett food chain. The next year we'd be graduating to a new school for 7th-9th grade and I was delighted about the promise of a new future.

I found myself in Mr. John Ogle's homeroom class. My dad had sold he and his wife a house, which Dad had personally built out of recreational curiosity about the industry. They shared a respectful rapport.

By the time I was Mr. Ogle's student, he was already enchanted with me by nature of the fact that he knew someone in my family tree. This time it was not a sibling, whose academic merits could already be pre-judged.

For his soft, effeminate features and delicate conversational skills when he was kindly disposed to you, Mr. Ogle could be a terrific disciplinarian if you fell out of his favor. We didn't have many male teachers so when we did, we heard terrifying parental authority in their tone. Everyone shaped up and stopped whatever activity Mr. Ogle found displeasing.

I never acted out in any way in his classroom, not even for the prankster's heart I was developing in my formative years. We would be changing classes once again that year, even more so than in fifth grade. The school was trying to prepare us for the constant switching we'd be doing our upcoming year. After succumbing to Mr. Ogle's high expectations every class we had with him, moving on to a new instructor was like letting the belt out after Thanksgiving dinner. Everyone could breathe again.

The first day we officially switched classes, I met a lovely woman who looked to be in her forties, stylish and very motherly. Her smile gave me a comfort that I'd not known with any previous teachers. I trusted her instantly.

"Hello, class. My name is Mrs. Kupiszewski." Was I supposed to say gesundheit or God Bless You?

I supposed her name sounded like coop-uh-chess-key. I wanted to call her coop-uh-zoo-ski, however. My rule is, when in doubt, pronounce it like it looks. I knew it was important to get a person's name correct. It mattered. I learned that when my sister married and her last name changed into a syllabic nightmare. I vowed to get my teacher's name correct.

Before anyone could speak a word, she followed it up with, "You can just call me Mrs. Kupp." Coop. I heard that correctly. Easier. Already she was encouraging us to work at our own comfort level. I liked her for that.

Mrs. Kupp took a sincere interest in all of us. She was very good at what she did and hardly ever raised her voice, but when she did, everyone halted. You didn't want to upset her. She was a mild Bruce Banner when she was in her usual frame of mind, but tick her off and you suddenly encountered the Hulk. I never had to experience her wrath, thankfully. She adored me and the feeling was mutual.

She had studied English and loved reading books to us. I remember clearly *Where the Red Fern Grows*. She was an animated reader and we gobbled up every word. Sitting in the middle of the room on a bar stool, she'd cross her legs daintily and respectfully open the pages that captivated our minds and emotions. It was Mrs. Kupp who got me interested in S.E. Hinton books. She read several of those to us during our stay in her classroom.

I'm unsure how it initially happened, but Mrs. Kupp discovered my passion for writing. I wrote all of the time. Journals, short stories and assignments for class, I attacked with a vigor few students showed toward the art. My thesaurus was my best friend. I craved language and better ways to convey the stories I wanted to tell. I was working on a novel that I took just as seriously as my studies when Mrs. Kupp offered to edit my work. If I would stay after class and allow her to give feedback, she was willing to indulge me her gift of proper grammar. I was thrilled. She treated me like a real writer and that's what I'd innately discovered I was destined to be.

I'd meet with her nearly daily and she'd masterfully critique my work. She was careful with me in her analysis, always encouraging and helpful even when she'd point out a better way to say something. I loved her for it.

I also loved that Mrs. Kupp tended to overlook my mischief. I really appreciated that indulgence. One day in her class, I noticed that my buddy Julie, who sat behind me, had her feet planted firmly on my chair. It was comfortable for her and I didn't mind at all because Julie was something special and I knew it even then. She was always in a good mood and laughed effortlessly at most things. She didn't take herself too seriously. Physically, Julie resembled a modern work of art. She had what Mom would call a china doll face. Julie was popular and fun and I knew she could take a joke. It's why I didn't hesitate to prank her that afternoon. While Mrs. Kupp was stirring the class for an activity, I noted that Julie's shoes were characteristically untied. I reached back and tied her laces to my chair. She let me. We were both laughing hysterically when I opted to scoot my chair up and Julie hopelessly splattered onto the floor behind me.

"Lisa!" she giggled, somehow surprised.

"What's the matter, Julie?" I asked serenely.

Mrs. Kupp saw the commotion and with a mother's delicate warning said, "Now girls."

I helped Julie get unhooked from my chair and we collected ourselves enough to pay attention. We both loved that Mrs. Kupp let us play.

Outside of class, I'd often see Mrs. Kupp and her husband jogging in town or walking their dogs. I'd see them nesting on their porch swing at their riverside home and I'd always take a moment to say "hello." Often, Mrs. Kupp invited me in and we'd talk like old friends.

I had already established myself as a good student by the time I told Mrs. Kupp the news that my brother had gone out on a date with her daughter. Thankfully, I no longer stood on my siblings' academic backbones. I had established my scholastic good standing all on my own. Nonetheless, I held my breath as Mrs. Kupp evaluated the news. Mark was taking classes to attend nursing school at this point and transforming into a responsible young man right before our family's eyes. When Mrs. Kupp determined he was a worthy prospect, I was relieved. Finally, a sibling stood solidly on *my* reputation. He should thank his lucky stars that I had a good one.

My mom liked the Kupps. She worked with Colonel Kupp and had enjoyed meeting Mrs. Kupp at parent-teacher conferences. Of course, it helped that Mrs. Kupp spoke nothing but kind words about me and my performance. Those reviews would continue even into the eighth grade, for Mrs. Kupp was transferring to our new school.

Mrs. Lauxman was transferring as well. I couldn't wait to tell Mom the good news…

MRS. ELSEA

East Junior High School had previously been Leavenworth High School, at least when my parents were attending classes there. The building held an antiquated charm and hallways full of memories for both of my parents. East, for me, was simply a closer walk from home and a chance to improve my sleeping skills. Until I found out that band would be held one hour before school. So much for the notion of rest.

My first obstacle in 7th grade was getting from the band annex to the school on time. It was only a few blocks away, but by the time I inserted my spit cleaner into my saxophone and crammed sheet music and accessories into its case, I had to haul ass with a backpack and my instrument to get to class. Marching days were worse, but then concert band day wasn't a piece of cake from that distance, either. I played the upright bass in concert band. Try hauling that home and then racing to get to school on time.

Once in the vicinity of our actual school, we had three floors to navigate between. Art in the basement, English on the second floor, third floor for biology, back down to the second floor for social studies and the nightmare jig jagging was just beginning. The gym was centrally located, but this was our first year of showering together and that awkwardness held everyone back a few minutes. I showered with my gym clothes on to save time and humiliation. Ms. Nielson, our gym teacher, never appreciated it, but she waited until I grew more comfortable before grading me on my shyness.

The higher the grade, the more survival skills you needed to beat the clock. Since this was our first year and we were essentially still little kids, everyone cut us some slack.

I was ready to face my new school, even with all of its hardships. I did miss my elementary school classmates. We were dispersed throughout the city. Some kids were going to Catholic junior highs and some to West Junior High, East's arch rival. I only knew West Junior High students because I played sports with them in the summer.

The most fascinating people to me were the new students infiltrating from the military base. I loved that they came from so many distant locations and I could learn about places I had only dreamed of exploring. The blended classrooms were intoxicating to me. I couldn't wait to see how I fared in the expanded learning environment.

Though I had many empowering teachers at East, I found my best ally in a teacher named Mrs. Elsea. She was an elfish young woman with a pixie haircut and glasses. I didn't know how I felt about her at first. In matters of education, she was rather pedantic. I hadn't discovered that intensity level since Miss Busey. I hoped Mrs. Elsea didn't play the piano. To my relief, she taught my favorite class, English. I had to engage her with all my might. She held the keys to my future aspirations of being an author.

Mrs. Elsea's class was second hour. Whether it was sleep deprivation or her sternness, I crumbled into submission in her class. Ornery as I was, I didn't trust that she had a sense of humor and I didn't have the energy for practical jokes anyway. Running between classes was exhausting. If the labyrinth layout of our classrooms was strategic, kudos. It worked. Schools should really consider renovating a defunct airline terminal if they want to give you an even better workout. And being able to run from one end to another would be an applicable life skill. Periodically, Mrs. Elsea could stand at a terminal gate yelling, "No running in the halls!" Mrs. Kupp and Mrs. Lauxman would be inside the former gifts shops hawking their wares. "Textbooks! Get your textbooks here!" Miss Busey could overtake the intercom for some rousing rendition of some crap no one understood. The possibilities were endless.

Mrs. Elsea was an effective teacher and I grew to really honor her approach. She was strict, but she was fair and for a child like me who respected both energies, I understood her and excelled in her class.

It wasn't until the end of my eighth grade year, though, that Mrs. Elsea and I sealed a bond that no other teacher could ever trespass.

I was waiting near a crosswalk of a busy four-lane highway which bordered the school. The rain had just started to pick up when a gentleman driving a pickup truck stopped and waived me across. I checked the traffic flow and didn't see any cars. I started to dart across the street, turning briefly to wave at the man, when a woman driving a formidable Cadillac sped up the other side of the truck and hit me. Obviously, neither the truck driver nor I saw her. And she definitely didn't see me.

I didn't remember any of the details myself. I instantly went into shock from the moment the bumper met my leg. I was later told that the force snapped my fibula. I had flipped into the air and the Cadillac caught me coming down. I smashed into the windshield, leaving my body's impression, and crashed onto her hood before rolling off the vehicle. I lay a bloody heap on the wet pavement of the well traveled and busy thoroughfare called 4th street.

It was the last day of my eighth grade year. We had been let out of school early, but there were no flashing lights to indicate this. Those came after my accident when my dad battled the city for their installation.

With finals complete, I had big plans. I was going to play video games with my friends at a restaurant across the street from my school. Later that night I intended to babysit another friend's younger brother. I was excited.

Once I saw the man in the truck wave to me and I made my move, my world went instantly black. I awakened with a blinding light in my face. "Where am I?"

"You're in the hospital. You've had an accident." My mom was by my side with a hand clamped over mine. She gripped me tighter in her worry.

I considered the events that came before. "Did I finish school?"

Mom checked her watch and gauged from the time of day that I probably had, "Yes, I believe you did."

"Did I take my finals?"

"I assume so."

I did a quick algebraic formula in my head. $3x=15$, so $x=5$. With that little test, I instinctively knew that I didn't have brain damage and I'd be okay.

The doctor arrived with a needle the size of my forearm and told me he'd be placing it in my forehead. "You have two large cuts and I'm going to sew them together. Just relax and count back from 10."

I got to 8, saw the needle coming at me and passed out.

The first few nights I spent vomiting the stress from my body in the intensive care unit. Kind nurses held buckets for me and gave me sponge baths, all the while turning away well meaning friends.

In my sequestered, healing environment, I heard all sorts of stories about what had supposedly happened to me. I was mummifed in a full body cast in one version. That was my personal favorite. I was on death's door clinging for life in another. One pervading sentiment based on all of the stories was that I was being prayed for fervently.

Many loved ones were lining up to see me through this tragic accident. Teachers dropped in to be sure I was alive and would survive this ordeal. Mrs. Kupp brought me a stuffed hospital dog for my friends to sign while I was yet in the ICU. She had already signed it.

Mrs. Lauxman showed up at the hospital, too. She was quiet. I knew that quiet very well. It reflected a penetrating concern where no words seemed enough.

All of my friends stopped in. No one could believe what had happened.

I could see the worry on my loved ones' faces, each and every one. I appreciated their concern.

I believed God saw me through it. I was out of the hospital in a matter of days and home recuperating all summer. I was bummed that I wouldn't get to play softball or tennis, but I championed my way through it. I had questions, though. Questions about the accident that no one could answer, at least not until I returned to school.

Mrs. Elsea sought me with purpose my first day back for ninth grade. She had been concerned all summer about me and wanted to let me know it immediately. She grabbed onto my arm and marched me into her classroom.

"I was there when you had your accident," she confessed. "If you have any questions, I will tell you."

She left it up to me in case the trauma of it was too great to bear.

"I want to know what happened," I admitted.

She checked my expression to be sure. Sensing my need to know, she began. "I was in the restaurant across the street getting lunch when I heard someone scream, 'Oh my God, she's been hit.'"

Mrs. Elsea looked down and restlessly fidgeted. I didn't say a word.

"I knew instantly that it was a student. I dropped my sandwich and ran outside yelling, 'Call 911!'" She measured every detail of the story and meted it out in small bites, either so I could digest it or so she wouldn't lose her nerve.

"I saw you lying in the street and I was heartsick because I knew it was you. I ran over to you and knelt down. You were bleeding profusely from the deep gashes in your forehead and I knew I needed to stop the bleeding." She paused to get clear about the sequences of events, adding all details and letting me sort out the relevant ones. I could tell this had traumatized her, too.

She continued her story by naming a young hoodlum that was walking past. "I screamed at him to give me his t-shirt. He hesitated and I just yelled, 'Give it to me. Now.' He took it off and threw it to me and I dabbed your blood and held pressure on it." I had never seen Mrs. Elsea so pale as when she was retelling this story to me. Even as many times as she likely told the story, it was surreal in comparison to looking me in the eyes and telling me.

"Teachers were looking out the windows. Scared. They kept coming to the doors and staring outside. They were extremely worried. By then they knew it was you. The woman that hit you was hysterical. No one could get her to calm down. She was terrified. Someone took her inside the school, trying to help soothe her rattled nerves."

I felt sorry for the lady. I always had from the beginning. I can't imagine how she felt.

Mrs. Elsea started naming all of the teachers who expressed concern. Some I'd had for classes, some not. I was moved by their compassion.

"Mrs. Yates kept coming to the door and then wandering in a daze down the hallways saying, 'Did you hear what happened to Lisa?' A lot of us were walking in a daze. We just couldn't believe it."

I had known Mrs. Yates for years. Her daughter was in my grade and I really liked her. Having Mrs. Yates for a teacher was like having another mom. I loved her.

I lost myself into the silence between Mrs. Elsea and myself. Finally, I hit on the question I most wanted to know. "Did I say anything or was I completely unconscious? I don't remember anything."

"Oh yes, you were awake. You were crying and you just kept screaming, 'It hurts!' You were in so much pain."

Mrs. Elsea had given me all the information she had and I

could tell she was spent. "I'm just glad I have you in my class this year. I can't tell you how glad I am that you're with us."

I reassured her in the best way I knew how, "I'm okay, Mrs. Elsea. And…thank you."

We had a glorious year together. She let me design her seating chart. It was our little secret. My best friend and I told her who didn't like one another and she placed them right next to each other to avert any unnecessary chatter. She allowed my best friend and me to sit together, providing that we honored our pact of silence. We did and stayed camped by one another all year.

A few years after my accident, Mrs. Elsea retired from teaching. She was very young and relatively new to the profession, but she wanted to operate a bed and breakfast in the quaint town she called home. I understood. In a way, I wondered if my accident had anything to do with it. Life events like that scare the best of us into living out our deepest passions. Maybe the trauma of it was just too much.

**

With years, comes more farcical versions of the tragedy. I was in college when the topic surfaced yet again. Riding home from a night out with my brother and niece, Mark was explaining to his daughter how careful you must be when crossing the street.

"Ask your Aunt Lisa," he laughed.

"Not this again," I laughed with him.

He stared into her innocent little face and said, "She got hit by a car crossing the street!"

"She did?" Ashley was shocked. She and my sister's oldest were less than a year old when the accident happened. Now old enough to cross streets themselves, everyone was getting the memo of my wreck. Mark took it to an exaggerated level.

"She sure did!"

We were all riding in the front cab of his truck when he whipped off onto the shoulder of an exit ramp.

"It happened just like this."

Mark checked for traffic, threw his truck in park and leaped out, running across the road. Ashley was already laughing when he stuck his thumb in his mouth and began skipping back toward us. When he was in full view of the windshield, he turned his head toward us and popped his eyes open in mock surprise.

When he jumped back in, we were all shrieking with laughter. "And that's how it happened, Ashley. Don't let her tell you any different."

"Ashley, I was 14 years old and far from skipping and sucking my thumb."

Mark shook his head contrarily. "Ash, I'm your father, listen close. She still sucks her thumb."

Everything I said about him growing into a responsible adult, I take it back.

CRAPPER CHRIS

A boy I'll call Chris in a class taught by a teacher I'll call Mrs. Stone, was a little asshole. Every class has one. Some have more than one. In seventh grade, Chris was competing for the title and it was looking like he was going all the way.

This kid knew everything. About everything. And everyone. Better than they knew themselves. No one really liked him. I kidded myself that I could tolerate him, but truthfully, he irritated me.

He was a smart ass to every student and for teachers, a nightmare. His behavior was an indictment of reckless parental indulgence. Punishments, for him, were mere suggestions.

Incorrigible. Unruly. Vapid. You name a term and he fit the bill.

He was constantly clicking the bands on his braces and speaking with the smacking voice of a kid with too much saliva caked on his tongue.

"Get a drink!" students would protest. Smiling, Chris would

continue clacking his way through class, asking questions, just for effect. He was a study in irreverence.

By the time Christmas break rolled around, he was the kid even the most polite children avoided. I was one of them. No one wished him a Merry Christmas. Most children wished that Santa would just crap down his chimney and leave. Take that lump of coal, you little hellion.

I was conflicted. Something about knowing that everyone shunned him near the holiday of cheer, made me sad for him. I was taught to find the good in everyone by my compassionate mother. Often I'd wind up rationalizing bad behavior in order to achieve that end. Our last day of school before Christmas break perfectly illustrated the tilting scale.

I saw Chris standing in front of the ornate public library near East Junior High. He was leaning against the payphones near the entry steps. I had to pass by him on my way home and he'd already seen me. I decided to extend an olive branch.

"Merry Christmas, Chris." I didn't overemphasize it with any exaggerated joy. It was quick and to the point.

"Lisa!" He motioned me towards him. I figured he'd do the decent thing and return my wish. "Come here. Someone's on the phone for you."

I knew it was a lie. I played along anyway.

When I put the phone up to my ear, I felt a clinging wetness dripping from my ear lobe. Chris was pointing and laughing.

When I placed a finger to my ear, a globule of dense spit fell into my hand. He had hawked a big one into the receiver and waited for a victim. Lucky me.

I was pissed. I chastised him and walked away with a furious, "No wonder no one likes you."

I fumed all Christmas break. My mom tried to console me, but it was futile. I refused to look for the good in Chris any longer. I plotted my entire Christmas break. I knew it wasn't the most spiritual thing to do, but I wanted revenge.

Lucky for me, my birthday always fell on the first day our classes resumed. I had planned to bring cupcakes. When all of the cupcakes had been decorated, but one, I slipped into my mom's bedroom and snuck a half full box of Ex-Lax tablets from her top dresser drawer. When my mom turned away from the stove, I threw some into the boiling homemade frosting and stirred them up. I iced the last cupcake myself and marked it with a certain color candle and fruity Lifesaver, also a distinct color. I wanted to be sure to identify it right away.

My best friend at the time was the only person who knew my plan. I arranged it that way so that she would hand out the cupcake. I figured it would be less suspicious.

When the time came and Mrs. Stone asked if I'd like to share my birthday treats, I noticed that the entire class was carefully examining the cupcakes. I turned to my best friend. Of course, she'd blabbed. This was too promising to not let everyone share in the moment.

As I passed out my birthday goods, students would confidentially ask me if theirs was laced, too. I told them that only one had been tampered with and I knew exactly which one and for whom it was destined. They relaxed. The focus shifted to Chris. My best friend handed out the tainted treat and he feverishly removed the wrapper.

"Why is everyone staring at me?" he whined. That voice was grating, even now when victory was at hand.

Everyone ate their cupcakes and licked the crumbs from their shirts and desks.

Chris inhaled his in a matter of bites. "Are there any more?" Oh, I wish I had known.

My entire class monitored Chris all day. Pint-sized informants would report back to me on his progress. Fifth hour would be the first time I'd seen him since the assault began.

We were a few minutes into science class with Mr. Ball (no need for an alias moniker there), when Chris sliced his arm into the air. Without permission, he interrupted class and urgently announced, "Mr. Ball, I have to go to the bathroom." He leaped up and started toward the door.

"Now wait just a second, Chris."

"I can't." He grabbed the back of his white jeans and held on tight, hoping to delay Montezuma's Revenge.

Chris left school that day with only one hour left to go. We didn't see him the following day, either. I never spoke a word of it. I didn't need to, just getting him back was enough. Further, I'd have been in some hot water myself trying to explain that one.

Near the end of the year, my little boyfriend was embroiled in an intellectual tug-of-war with Chris. When he'd had enough, my boyfriend unleashed his fury with a call back to my previously secret revenge.

"Well, at least I didn't shit my pants when I ate Lisa's cupcakes."

I saw Chris's contorted face as the details unfolded. He was pale and looked like he was contemplating a revisit to his restroom sanctuary all over again. I tried to ignore them, but found myself with both Chris and my boyfriend flanking me.

"Tell him. Tell him about the Ex-Lax," my boyfriend demanded. I glared at him. How could he tattle after all of the months I'd retained that information? Everyone else had remained respectfully mum on the topic and most of them thanked me.

"She wouldn't do that," Chris insisted. "She's too nice."

I lowered my voice and leaned in. "Don't ever underestimate me again." He was stunned. "You should have never spit in that phone receiver."

The following year, Chris's military family had transferred. They were only stationed in Leavenworth a year. I'm thinking for Crapper Chris, one year was long enough. It certainly was for the rest of us. I bet he yet wonders if being an asshole was worth it.

I ultimately confessed to my mom what I'd done. She often asks, "Do you ever feel bad for doing it?"

My answer has always been, "No." In recent years, I've reconsidered.

I did learn a valuable lesson from the experience. Revenge is a dish best served in a cold, porcelain bowl. Sometimes that bowl backs up.

MRS. WALL

My mom was mortified. My dad was mad. Even my brother weighed in with his own embarrassment. I didn't know what to think.

"You let her in here? In our house?" My dad threw objects around in a rage.

"Wow!" My brother shook his head. His exclamation wasn't one of excitement, but of a perceived colossal failure on my part. Typical judge first, listen later reaction.

The only one who owned her humiliation and yet didn't project it onto me was my mom. Mom hurried about, tidying up. It was too late. "Oh, I wish you hadn't done that. I would've cleaned up for her first." My mom was frazzled with post-traumatic cleaning disease.

I was dismayed that everyone pointed an accusatory finger at me. What was I supposed to do?

Mrs. Wall was my ninth grade gym teacher and an assistant volleyball and track coach at East. She came in the year I would be leaving East Junior High and made herself at home. She was simply dreamy. Bouncy blond curls pushed back most days with a fashiobable barette or hair band, pastel blue eyes and a body built by a volleyball scholarship. She was fresh out of college and eager to learn the ropes of teaching. We weren't that far apart in age and that fostered a relatable level of interest. She didn't hesitate to co-mingle her extracurricular activities with her students.

"How about we celebrate your graduating to high school with a pick up game of sandlot volleyball?" she asked the most nimble of our female athletes. A few girls, who hadn't spent any time with an instructor outside of class, withheld their acceptance initially. I was eager to take her up on the invitation. What were they waiting for? This was the opportunity of a lifetime. We were getting the chance to play our coach.

"It's just that I haven't played competitively in so long and I really miss it," Mrs. Wall presented her case. "You girls are in such great shape, I'm sure you'll challenge me and I need that." Her eyes pleaded with a barely suppressed excitement. She was a young woman who never got turned down. I would discover those girls in my life from that point forward. By nature of blessed genes and a vigorous enthusiasm, they powered their way through every goal they envisioned. Mrs. Wall would be no different. She would not be denied.

The girls bartered for time with the classic, "I'll have to ask my mom first." That statement seemed fair and Mrs. Wall relented for the moment.

As it ended up, all of us showed up at the designated meeting spot on the steps in front of the school. We piled into Mrs.

Wall's Toyota Tercel as we'd done throughout the track season.

At times, she'd pack as many as ten kids into her car on our way to track and haul us, axles dragging, the brief distance to Abeles Field where we practiced. With a car, it was brief, anyway. Abeles was quite a hike, otherwise. And like everything else, we were being timed.

Mrs. Wall felt sorry for us and helped us out. She'd fire up her car and yell, "Anyone want a ride?" Everyone bolted for the passenger seat, but hardly anyone made it. Sometimes you had a stick shift up your ass and sometimes it was suctioned to the hatchback window. You never knew where you'd land when you dove in. Once inside, she'd turn the radio on to a popular channel. In no time, we'd find ourselves singing the top 40 hit song by Nu Shooz, "I Can't Wait" or in our case, "I Can't Wait to Get Out of This Car."

Sandlot volleyball day, we drove to a city park miles from our homes, comfortably seated on top of one another. It was roomy in comparison to our track day travels.

We played full out the entire afternoon: digging, diving, pummeling, setting, spiking and serving. The sun beat down on our sweat soaked skin and the sand pervertedly found every orifice and camped there waiting to become a pearl.

When our games wound down and our mitochondria had churned out its last bit of expendable energy, we stopped. A few parents showed up to take their little darlings home. They were likely concerned about their girls hanging out with the gym teacher. They'd heard stories. Once they saw Mrs. Wall, I could see their relieved and yet confused expressions. Even sprinkled liberally with sand, she was stunning. Most gym teacher stories people heard involved a gorilla morphed linebacker who checked out their girls in the shower. It was a myth.

The group had dwindled some, but there were still quite a few of us to take home. Mrs. Wall, Tamie as she insisted we call her, turned to the rest of us with a new mission. She rested hopeful eyes upon me, "So ladies, does anyone have a shower I can use?"

Most of the other girls, particularly my African American friends, went momentarily speechless. Finally one girl spoke up, "How would I ever explain a white Barbie doll in our shower to the rest of my family?" With that logic, the rest of the girls begged out right away.

It didn't matter. Tamie never really looked to any other person for the favor than me. Her eyes were fixated on mine from the moment she suggested it. I anticipated it would be me. We had shared a lot of personal stories that year and I fashioned she considered me a friend.

"Oh, I don't know," I started to say. My mom and dad were at work so that would've been okay, but my brother could come home any time.

I wasn't ashamed of our modest home. I suspected a few of the other girls didn't share my comfort level.

Before I could come to a full conclusion, Tamie offered her side, "You see, I have to drive a long distance home and I don't really want to do that with all of this sand everywhere. It will get all over my car and it's difficult to clean out."

"But...you'll have sand in it anyway when you take us home. I have it everywhere," an angelic black girl reasoned. I had thought the exact same thing.

Tamie hadn't anticipated the logic. Would she allow it to foil her plan? Out of the question. "I just mean it's itchy and uncomfortable and I'd rather be clean for my drive home to my husband."

Something in all of us stirred. It didn't feel exactly true, but we couldn't quite put a finger on it.

We stood around, but she made no motion for her car. This needed a resolution or we wouldn't be going home anytime soon.

"I need to get home," one of the girls, who had emphatically refused her right from the start, piped up.

I caved. "Well, I guess you can bathe at my house. I don't have a shower, though." I hoped it would change her mind.

"Perfect! Thank you so much, Lisa!" Her eyes lit up and she was smiling at me like a poster child for excellence. I was the one she wanted and now she had me. She was ecstatic. I felt sick to my stomach with worry. Would I get in trouble for this? I wasn't much of an odds player. I always just assumed Dad would be pissed no matter what the occasion. Assumption or not, it was ordinarily the case.

Mrs. Wall dropped a few girls off at their homes, but the rest she left on the doorsteps of East Junior High. They were walking home. I presumed they didn't want her to know where they lived lest she needed a KOA at a later date.

I instructed her to my home a few blocks away. When we pulled into the driveway, I could hear the ticking of her car's hot engine similar to the ticking clock in my house counting down the minutes until my parents arrived home. Mark's car was not there so he must've had to stay late at his college campus. I put the key in the lock and opened the door.

"It might be a little messy." I didn't know her standards for upkeep so it was hard to tell how she'd categorize it. Tamie assured me that she didn't care at all about the condition of our house.

It's not like Mom didn't try. She cleaned thoroughly every Saturday with plenty of Pine-Sol and other random chemical agents. I vacuumed almost daily when I arrived home from school. And dishes were usually done and put away. There was clutter, however. A lot of it was my dad's, but he bitched like it belonged to everyone else. There was always some random crap lying around that no one especially loved, but stored anyway out of obligation to a gift giver. My dad kept a lot of what he called "antiques" for their perceived value. My mom gently rectified that notion. Even though she would use less abrasive language, "It's all crap," was implied.

"Don't throw it away, it'll be worth something some day," my dad insisted.

"It's a pen and it doesn't work," I'd argue flatly.

"I said leave it."

And that was always the final word. Thus another useless item taking up space.

Tamie walked respectfully into our home. I can't imagine what she saw. I saw familiarity and memories. I guessed she probably saw a sizable open cabinet stacked with mismatched bowls and opened packages of food, carpet worn thread bare with use and knickknack overload because my Mom loved us enough not to part with our gifts. Ah. Home.

The real terror lie beyond the bathroom door. I opened it and saw a jungle of pantyhose hanging all over the place, clinging to one another like veins. I forgot it was Mom's day to dry her "all togethers" as she called them. What shocks me even now is that it never occurred to me to take them down. I spread them out of the way like I was opening a stage curtain and showed Tamie to her bathroom haven. I never checked to see if anyone left anything undesirable in the soap. I didn't rinse the tub. I handed Mrs. Wall a towel and a washcloth and left her to her business. She handed me her clothes and allowed me to rinse them out and dry them for her. It was the least I could do.

It didn't occur to me until later that she had a certain look in her eyes. The same look the rest of my family had when I told them, "Hey, my teacher just left. I let her take a bath here after our volleyball match."

"You what?" my dad bellowed.

My mom ran to the bathroom and yanked her hose down. "Oh, Lisa."

My brother was smirking and doubting my sensibilities all at once.

"I don't think she minded. She just wanted to rinse off before her long drive home."

"How far away does she live? Canada?" my brother mocked.

I answered with a location in the Kansas City area.

"That's not even a half hour away. Fifteen minutes. Tops." My brother barked.

I didn't get the big deal.

**

Mrs. Wall and I spoke every time I came back to visit East. She had finally settled into her job and likely never asked another student for a shower. Still, it never quite made sense to me what the whole incident was about. I always thought it was innocent.

Years later, a lesbian friend cornered me when I told the story with the same nonchalance I had in youth.

"Oh my gosh. Really? You could have had the coveted teen-age love story. Everyone wants to shag their gym teacher, but hardly anyone ever actually gets the chance. What were you thinking? She needed a shower to wash the sand off? You believed that? Wow. You missed out."

I argued for Tamie's virtue, "Tamie was married."

"Oh, like that ever stops someone from acting on their sexual preferences."

"She was happily married and I was a teen-ager. We were friends."

"You could have been better friends," my buddy laughed, rolled her eyes and wandered away.

Wow…

MS. B

I met one of my best friends while in ninth grade. Ms. B was an outspoken, witty and supportive New York transplant who taught Geometry. She was mid-30's and cute as a baby with her wide, expressive brown eyes that lit up when she laughed. And she did that often. She had a way with words and a fashion consciousness that reflected her big city roots. She also had an accent that lent her a credible reputation for not accepting students' bullshit. She wasn't a bully in the classroom, far from it. She was caring and genuinely concerned with our learning.

Geometry was part of my advanced coursework curriculum and I took mastering it very seriously. It was tough for me. I'd spend hours trying to understand the math of paragraphs. Theorems. Ugh. I hated them. I did my best, though. It was the one class where my self-imposed rule of no free time until I finished my homework kept me from leisure activities for days on end.

And there was no one in my family who could help me grasp the subject matter. My mom informed me that she was an average student who really didn't understand a lot of the school work I had to take. "I paid attention and studied awfully hard, but I was just not blessed in school."

My mom informed me that her father patiently tried to help her on any given subject, but she just didn't enjoy it at all. Mom was a student who only wanted to study what she liked. Montessori was invented for children like her, but they didn't have that option where we lived.

When I'd ask for help with school projects that required creativity, she was a great help. When I'd get taxed to my frustrated max with difficult subjects, she'd defer me to another, "Ask your dad. He's smart and good with math."

My dad had my Nanny's gift of being able to do classic math in his head without rulers or calculators. However, abstract thinking such as geometry was not his gift.

"Mom used to do my homework for me," he admitted, "I had to work.

To put food on the table, everyone made sacrifices in his household. He worked to help support their family and when he didn't get around to homework, my grandma would help him.

Dad would puzzle over my geometry book and hand it right back. "No clue."

Mom and he both assured me I'd get it. I'd spend hours soaking my textbook in tears because I didn't get it. Inevitably, I'd wind up staying after school with Ms. B letting her explain it to me.

Mrs. Brandenburg, who shortened her name for our class's benefit, would pore over theorems for hours and work through problems with me. I was clinging to my A in her class, but it wasn't without incredible effort.

Throughout our time together, she'd enlighten me about her life. She was an enthralling woman and we built our friendship slowly, share by share. I think it's why it was sealed in stone that we'd be friends forever.

Even though I had insight into her personal life to base my evaluation on, I fully understood the kind of person Ms. B was by nature of how she treated me on one of my worst days. I had received a C on one of her tests. For all of my studying efforts, it tarnished what I saw as a nearly flawless academic record to that point. I'd fallen in my eyes, that day when my world crumbled under the grade C.

I fled the class, tormented by inadequacy, and childishly hid in the girls' restroom. I figured she'd find me. I don't know how I knew, I just did. While everyone went to lunch, I sat in a stall with my feet up, crying. I had tried so hard and failed. I was brutal on myself. I wish I could say it was the final time I treated myself so abusively, but it wasn't.

In my household, I was expected to be perfect. Not in school work, necessarily. Mark had blown that expectation when he rebelliously strolled through school to collect his diploma. Even he was making more efforts these days, though, to get into nursing school. When he'd stumble in a class, my dad would grumble, "You'll be flipping burgers a long time, if you don't pass these tests." Then he'd cut Mark a tuition check and leave.

My mom never pressured us on anything. She'd express her pride when we succeeded and her empathy when we did not. My dad didn't pressure me with school because I typically did well. He'd look over my grades, tell me he was proud of me and dig into his wallet to offer a financial reward. I'm sure he had plenty to spare since he'd saved so much on my brother's early academic disappointments.

On issues other than school, Dad was a downright bully with me. He insisted I get things right the first time, even if I hadn't been exposed to the task before. It was unrealistic. I remembered when I was little being terrified to eat out. I'd spill drinks and get yelled at for making a mistake. I was a bundle of nerves when I'd subsequently be asked to dine out. I'd focus so hard on not spilling my drink that I'd wind up knocking it over anyway in my overattentiveness. There was never any patience expressed for mistakes.

Despite my efforts to avert it, the trickle down of perfectionism melted into my own personal armor. Mark's, too. Mark became the guy who wanted everything done right the first time and with anal, nitpicky detail. I followed suit.

For anyone paying attention, that day I received a C was a reflection of my conflicting home values.

"Lisa?" I heard the concern in Ms. B's voice. "Lisa, I know you're in here. Please, come out."

I was busted and there wasn't anywhere to run. I opened the squeaking bathroom door, unraveled myself from the fetal ball I'd rolled myself into and made myself present.

She stared at me with a serious look on her face. "Lisa, there is nothing wrong with a C. It doesn't weight your entire grade. It's just one grade. You still have an A in the class and you'll do better next test. I know you will."

I was stubbornly wiping tears away, trying desperately not to let her see me cry. It was a lost cause. Once I'd reached that phase, there was no stopping the flood. I was humiliated.

"I can't believe I got a C. It's my first one."

"Well, now the sting is off. You expect so much of yourself. Ordinarily I'd say it's good, but you've got to give yourself a break sometimes, too."

She was right. I knew she was right. I had grown to expect a lot of myself. No one was pushing me academically, but me.

I walked out of the restroom with Ms. B. She refused to leave without me.

I worked even harder and came back even stronger in my next tests and secured my A in the class. I ended the year by winning nearly every single academic award for the girls in my grade and took my place center stage to collect my trophies.

That summer, Ms. B asked if I wanted to take golf lessons with her. I would work with my brother painting houses most of the day and take a few late afternoon lessons with her. We were solid partners in the learning environment. I found that with my tennis, volleyball and softball swings mastered, I had to change up my technique to have an effective golf swing. It was awkward at first, but I was soon skilled at the basics and playing with an edge I'd not known I possessed in the sport.

It was a long drive back to my house from the country club so Ms. B and I made good use of the time. We often spoke candidly about my future. She was interested in me as a student and friend. I returned the friendship in full.

She told me that as a young woman living in New York, she had a boyfriend that she was convinced she'd marry one day, but he died while serving in Vietnam. She always thought I'd marry my best friend Matt one day. Years later, when Matt passed, she shared her deep empathy with me. It likely brought up so many memories of her own.

She would often tell me that she never forgot her first love. She explained that she ultimately married a guy that provided her a son, whom she adores, but the marriage didn't work out.

I learned about her passion for motorcycles and was intrigued by her tales of Sturgis. More intrigued by the fact that she could hold a motorcycle up by herself. She was 98 pounds soaking wet if she was an ounce, but she was mighty and unperturbed by the daunting task of balancing a throbbing pulse of metal. She had remarried a guy named Wayne, who was a motorcycle enthusiast in his own right. Accountant by day, avid cyclist by night. Wayne and I learned that we had a mutual friend from an entirely different social circle and it linked us in a friendship as well. Much as I adored Wayne and knew Carol took his last name, I never stopped calling her Ms. B. It has amused her throughout the seasons of an almost 30-year friendship.

The perk of knowing someone so well is that now when we see one another, we can dish on the students and teachers we once knew. She had mentioned when I was a ninth grader that she was in a war with one of my classmates. She wouldn't name the kid. Her rule with me back then was that she'd never tell me anything she'd experienced with any students until I was graduating from high school. It was respectful in a way that many students didn't deserve, but I honored her in that and never asked. When I had advanced to Leavenworth Senior High School, I'd periodically drop by East and check in. We'd share laughs for hours and tell stories, but never a word about her worst students. Finally, commencement arrived and within days, I found myself at East Junior High. I had questions.

"Are you graduated already?" she laughed.

"Do you need proof of my diploma?"

"No," she laughed harder.

As it turned out, she hated a boy I'll call Dan.

"So, cough it up. It's been four years. What did Dan do?"

Without a second's hesitation, she whips out, "He flashed me his little pecker."

"He did what!?!"

"Flashed me that tiny little thing. Sure did. Right there," she pointed to a plastic chair on the front row of her class, "in that spot."

"No way!" I believed her, but I was being dramatic. Dan. Who knew?

"Big shit storm," she continued. "Conferences. Reprimands. Accusations and denials." She shook her head.

"Why did he do it?"

"Because he's a little shit, that's why. I hate that kid."

I have always loved her honesty. What's funny is that Ms. B is the same now as she was then. I can rely on her to be the person she introduced me to right off. She's still outspoken, caring and humorous and she still, to this day, hates that little prick.

CAR WARS

The summer between East Junior High and my transfer to Leavenworth Senior High, I took driver's ed. Every day I walked the equivalent of ten miles uphill in the snow the whole way. Except it was a sweltering Kansas summer and the walk was flat, perilous from road construction with a mirage for a destination. By the time I reached the high school every day, I was drenched. It wasn't the sexy sweat of models, either. I looked like I'd baked in a rain storm. My hair was glued to my forehead in a way that made me look like a 1950s adolescent boy. Hardly anyone noticed. My class shared the interchangeable Garanimals appeal of sweat induced, matching fashion. Everyone wore shirts that looked like maps of the world with the perspiration lines accentuating our anatomical features, dividing and conquering new terrain as it trickled along. Our shorts hiked up just far enough that when we sat down everyone could observe each others' identical farmer's tans. The frigid air conditioning in our classroom felt refreshing for a moment before stiffening our clothes and numbing our senses.

The class didn't enthrall me any and I certainly couldn't absorb all of the traffic rules. I found the open road a better education.

"I won't tell Mom if you want to take your car out for a test drive," my co-conspirator brother offered one afternoon.

"OK. Let me get my keys."

Mark had already been my true driving instructor for years. He let me ride his bicycles and never complained when they came back bent or scratched. In exchange for privacy with his girlfriend, he threw his expensive snow skis outside and let a friend and me practice on the downhill slope of our alley, chattering the bottoms with gravel and ice. Motorcycle? Sure, I could give it a try. He stayed on the back to guide me. Even so, we almost hit a telephone pole. Boat? Well, that would come later. Once I figured out how to accelerate without standing the boat on end, I was much better at it. My first attempt, we nearly sunk it. Cars were different. Mark let me experiment in our driveway with the push button car he owned. I nearly took out the side of the house. With each bungled attempt at transportation, he kept my confidence and never told on me. Of course, his silence was not as virtuous as it seemed. We would have both paid dearly, if caught. Fact is, I drove nearly every car he owned from the time I was eleven years old on. It was our little secret. Much of the time, it was out of necessity. We worked together, mostly on construction sites, during the summers and since he had no one else to ask when he needed vehicles moved or rearranged for a job, he had to trust me. It all worked out.

"Let's go!" I ran out of the house with my keys and my freshly minted license.

"Oh, I'm not riding with you. I meant take it out on your own."

I was stricken with fear. I hadn't driven completely unsupervised yet. He read my reaction and reassured me, "You'll be fine."

I hesitantly opened the car door and hopped in. I did all of my checks, gained my composure and then released the gear shift. Mark waved and I drove away in the cautious, speed weary manner of the elderly.

I turned the stereo on low to minimize distractions. I wasn't five miles from my house when I decided to turn around and come back. Mom would be getting off work and I didn't want to meet her in the driveway.

I chose a construction site for my turn around. The concrete hadn't been poured for the driveway yet and I could see the tracks that other vehicles had already made. I figured it would be a breeze. What I hadn't anticipated was the soft mud from the previous night's rain. I was stuck and there was no one around to help me. I vaguely remembered my dad telling me how to get out of just such a predicament, but it wasn't working. As Steve Winwood belted "Higher Love" from my stereo, I put the Ford Falcon in forward and then reverse, alternating rapidly, hoping to rock it out of the deep rut I'd landed in. The more I rocked the car, the further my tires plummeted into the earth. I turned the stereo up. It's a trick I would learn could soothe most vehicular situations.

"What's that noise?" a friend would ask.

"I don't know. Turn the stereo up." All better.

It wasn't better, however. I kept trying and singing and crying at this point. Finally, something gave way and my car lunged forward. I sped home. Well, as fast as the car would willingly go. I arrived in the driveway just before my mom got home. Mark stared at the mud pinstripes streaking the sides of the car. The tires were caked.

"What did you do?"

I explained as we both feverishly sprayed the car down with the garden hose. Mom arrived mere minutes after we finished. It was a close one.

I put that car through dozens of tests during my high school years. I learned that it wouldn't leap railroad tracks. Too heavy. I couldn't race anyone without cutting through parking lots. Too slow. I barely achieved one of the few speeding tickets I've ever received, while driving it.

"How does the car driving in the middle of two speeding cars get the ticket?" my brother had asked.

"When it's the only one that pulls over."

"Dummy," he laughed affectionately.

I made some mistakes driving, but I was in good company. Nearly every time I saw my friend Jamie on the road, he was pulled over with another car and a policeman. Accidents were a nearly monthly occurrence for him. Baffling that a local pharmacy employed him as a delivery driver and never fired him.

I enjoyed Jamie's reckless skills. He had a sports car that could play. My conservative classic could only be coddled in hopes that it wouldn't break down going the speed limit.

The only time Jamie scared me was when we were driving to a concert together an hour away and opted to race another car. He asked me first, but I could tell he really wanted to prove his car had what it took. Cue the *Rocky* theme song, I agreed.

"Buckle your seatbelt. If we wreck, we're going to be eating Datsun parts."

Even at 120 mph, the other car was pulling away. I had never driven that fast in my life. Every hair was tingling when we pulled into the concert venue. We made the hour drive in thirty minutes.

On the way home, something overheated and hot oil blasted underneath the dashboard on the passenger side, scalding my legs. He couldn't apologize enough.

"It's okay. At least I won't have to wax my legs for awhile." I joked because I didn't have any permanent injuries, but I was mindful of the costs of overindulgent joy riding.

My best friend Matt, whom I met my sophomore year, was a risky driver. He abused his Ford Escort with avidity. On a casual winter's day, he drove a friend and me down a boat ramp to challenge how far we could go toward the Missouri River's edge without going in. What he never considered was the ice beneath the thin layer of snow. The car slid out of control and rushed toward the frigid water. He braked, a mistake, and we were on a collision course with drowning. My friend in the backseat, trapped by the hatchback, was screaming and cussing him. Matt was shaken and furiously working the stick shift to keep us from being consumed by the fast approaching Muddy Mo.

I opened the passenger side door.

"What are you doing?" he panicked.

"Getting the fuck out," I spoke matter-of-fact. Fear had dissipated all emotions, but my survival instinct was crisply honed in. I was preparing to leap when he cried out.

"Wait!"

The tires caught pavement somehow and the car stopped just as the water lapped the white walls. He eased it up the incline to a clearing.

My friend lashed him with her insults. She was having an out-of-body experience of sorts, driven by adrenaline and fear. Her mouth kept moving, but she wasn't fully present.

"Don't you ever do something that stupid again," I warned him.

I learned valid lessons during my formative driving years. Never drive angry being a key one. Working out my frustration over a disagreement with a friend, I went for a drive. My car was top heavy and when I turned the steering wheel too quick, it tilted on its side and rolled along on two wheels. I nearly shit my pants as I saw the ground closing in on the driver's side. It finally settled back onto its quadrant of Firestones. I made a decision that day to work out or journal when I'm upset. Live and learn.

My senior year, my friends and I engaged in a little game we called "Car Wars." We would choose partners out of our group of friends and attempt to best one another in our creative decorating.

Sometimes it was Matt and me pulling pranks on Jamie. Sometimes Jamie and Matt would pair up. Often, I'd gather outsiders to help me get them.

"We just can't do anything that will peel away the finish," I made our one and only rule.

For every roll of toilet paper we'd use, I'd leave the empty, hollowed tubes stacked on the antenna so our victim knew with each and every one how much I cared. I would strip small pieces of the plushy pulp and place them in every vent hole on the hood. A few strips would be interwoven between wheel well holes. Famously, I'd wrap the entire car with toilet paper by having a partner in crime stand on the opposite side of the car. We'd toss the Charmin back and forth, rolling it first under the car and then over. I'd use shaving cream on the windows. If the person was really special to me, I'd leave Vaseline under the door handles. That's as bad I got with the whole idea. Matt and I applied all of these tactics for Jamie while his car sat defenseless in the school parking lot one Friday night. He was participating in marching band for our football team's away game. Arriving late, exhausted I'm sure, he didn't look forward to tearing off toilet paper, but at least it was a quick and painless ordeal.

I coerced my friend Christina to get Matt. We were heading to a movie when we saw Matt's car parked a block from the theater. It probably couldn't get any worse than coming out of a movie to find your car's windows completely covered with Oreo halves which we twisted apart, licked and stuck to every window. The licked suckers lining the hatchback were a nice touch, too. We stood guard waiting for him to leave the theater and shooing away a little kid who kept trying to eat the treats.

When Matt walked out with Jamie and saw the car, his face fell. I knew the look. It typically accompanied his favorite threat, which he always delivered with a sinister laugh, "I'm very vengeful and I'm very patient."

When Christina and I exited the theater a few hours later, I saw a shaving cream and coffee grounds mixture smeared on my windows. I couldn't see through the glass. Using the wipers only made it worse. It was, however, the only reason I saw the note that had been shoved underneath them. Inside the folded piece of notebook paper, in Jamie's handwriting, was an apology. They knew this was a bad one. The note, amidst its hugs and kisses, please-don't-be-mad flavor, had a five-dollar bill to clean up. It had to be Jamie. Matt would've never offered it in those days, the little sadist.

Jamie and I forked Matt's lawn in addition to decorating his car as penance for the movie theater escapade. Jamie felt guilty so he was easy to sway. Matt walked out of his house the following morning to mow the lawn and found hundreds of plastic forks standing at attention in his yard. Not to worry, he got his sweet revenge.

I hid my car at Christina's house when we were going out one Saturday night. I parked at the top of the hill from where her house actually rested. I figured no one would find it there. We drove around that night in Christina's car because she loved to cruise the local drag, 4th street, always wanting to see who was out and what was happening. We drove by the house of a guy she had a crush on all through high school. She'd squeal out the windows every time we passed by. I don't think he ever knew her devotion.

When we arrived back at her house, I could see the toilet paper waving in the wind like a flag. Matt.

"Oh no," she laughed.

My car was decorated end to end. There was whip cream and shaving cream on all of the windows, smashed down and sealed in by Saran Wrap. I also noted a yellowish substance swirled within the creams which I would later find out was Cheez Whiz. Coffee grounds were sprinkled on top of it all. The white walls were completely covered with white shoe polish, giving the appearance of powdered donuts. He even stole my signature move. I found a generous dollop of Vaseline slathered on every door handle and toilet paper to top off the masterpiece. All of the rolls lined the antenna with love.

Christina saw my face change. This was too far. I had a curfew and I was already running a few minutes late.

"I can't drive this car like this."

Christina couldn't go with me to clean it, but let me use her parents' phone to call my mom and explain that I'd be late. It was a nightmare to clean. It took well over an hour. Alone.

Matt admitted that he and seven other people he'd crammed into his car, spent a good hour decorating and then even longer waiting for me to show up and see it. When I didn't, he left.

Needless to say, Car Wars ended there.

WALRUS

I never remembered the woman's name. Everyone just called her Walrus. The nickname was just as much about her pear-shaped morphology as her unfortunate predisposition in looks to the silly creature. She wore shapeless floral dresses all year long and comfortable shoes that she hardly made use of. After her initial instructions, she sat behind her desk ignoring us for the remainder of the class.

Her inattentiveness was a gift, really. We were supposed to be learning about computers, but managed, instead, to wage paper ball wars every class period. Oh, we did our work, but every assignment lasted little more than fifteen minutes, at least for those of us who caught on quickly. The stragglers lingered at their hazy monitors all hour with little guidance from Walrus.

Every period, we'd rush through our class work and pretend to engage what was supposed to be silent study time. It always turned into mass chaos. Someone would lob paper wads at the boys I'll call Ralph and Ryan and it was on. Two outcasts against an entire class. I would have felt for them had they backed down in pitiful submission, but they fired back. Sometimes one or the other of them would even instigate it.

Since they were willing and active participants, guilt went right out the window on the wings of a paper snowball.

One day a troublemaker on the back row found the file cabinet unlocked. He fake yawned, reached back and located spools of clear masking tape. He passed them around. Everyone worked like Rosie the Riveter in the war effort.

"Wrap them tightly around the paper wad," someone from our camp commanded.

By the time we finished, we had circular paper bombs, potent as Ninja stars, that could knock you unconscious on contact.

Everyone waited for Walrus to turn around and on a whispered count of three, launched their weapons at the same time. The hail storm of paper balls descended upon Ralph and Ryan equally and left both of them laughing and wiping their stinging, pimpled skin.

When Walrus turned around, everyone camped in their textbooks with their heads bowed. The only evidence of our mischievousness was the unshaken snow globe scene of cheery children laughing, surrounded by snowy white paper pebbles.

I was fond of Walrus. On occasion she'd let me and a few other favorites skip her early morning class and go on a breakfast run to Burger King or Mickey D's. It was our choice. The only thing she asked was that we bring her some food. Feeling especially good one morning, we not only brought her breakfast, but kited the fake flowers from our table at Burger King. They were still in their vase. She was laughing with us when we set her table and produced the flowers.

"Ambiance," I offered.

Just before our last day of class, Walrus stepped out into the hall to speak with another teacher. We, of course, began a paper wad fight that would've scared anyone. Balls were zinging so fast in the air, you'd have thought we opened up the ceiling and just dumped them on top of ourselves. Tragically, one well fired wad sailed into the hallway right past Walrus, hit a wall and somehow landed at her feet. Neither teacher noticed and kept right on talking.

"Man, Walrus is clueless," a classmate observed.

The next day was it for her. She had given us an early final and was no longer obligated to stick around. Walrus was moving on to another school and we would be ending our sophomore year.

She walked into class that morning, grimacing. In a serious tone, she began a lecture I'd never forget. "Class, I just want you to know that all year I have put up with your antics." She walked to the door, peeked outside and with the coast clear, willed it shut. She wandered back to stand behind her desk. "I've overlooked every single paper ball fight you have had. You have gotten me in trouble with faculty and staff. You've now gotten me fired. I just want you to know before I go…" she reached down and opened the lower drawer of her desk "… that I'm sick of it. I've had enough." She cocked her arm back and fired a paper wad right at Ralph. It landed on his lip and ricocheted off. Bulls-eye. "Let the final paper ball fight begin," she was laughing. A hoax and a trap. I loved her creativity.

Shocked and elated all at once, we scattered around the room collecting our arsenal. Walrus had most of them in her desk drawer and was batting them around the room with intense speed and accuracy. Using her desk as a bunker, she hid behind it and let us have it, ducking countless paper balls which sailed over her head in retaliation. Sheets of paper could be heard being ripped out of spiral notebooks around the room. By the time we finished, the classroom was a disaster. Walrus had shown us that she was a fierce competitor. She walked out that day without looking back. Good for her.

DR. BOB

I found it unusual that we had a teacher who identified himself as a doctor. Even if other professors had earned the title, no one ever used it at the high school level. For a name that in some ways was less formal than Mr. So and So, it still had an air of propriety. He was anything, but proper.

Dr. Bob taught chemistry. I remember nothing of the class itself. I would be bombarded with the subject in college as a payback for my waning attention span in my advanced high school class.

What I do remember is Dr. Bob's playful attitude toward the rest of us. He mocked us constantly. When we'd do something he found sub par, he delighted in telling us so. Of particular amusement for him was the day he explained that our class would not be allowed to make touch paper.

"Thank your upper classmen for that. Somehow lining toilet seats with touch paper in hopes the pressure would ignite it, has bestowed their punishment on you. Your class, quite simply, can't be trusted."

Everyone moaned. We relished the idea of scaring our fellow

classmates with a fire in the hole, so to speak.

"We'll be good," we promised.

He rolled his eyes. "I've seen this bunch in action. Far too many pranksters in this group," he looked directly at the back row and specifically to my friends and me.

Prankster? Who me?

It wasn't exactly my ornery nature that called me into question. A friend of mine and I, let's call her Tracy because that's her name, were enjoying a beer one afternoon. Don't ask me which drunken soul loitering outside of a liquor store we overpaid to buy it for us. It could've been any number of them. It was most assuredly a stranger that we reasoned would be empathetic to our adolescent mischief.

We had exactly one beer which we shared. When we determined that we needed to throw the bottle out before buying some gum and heading home, we happened to drive through a friendly little neighborhood. It was near the Missouri River overlook. Beautiful older homes brushed elbows with one another over tightly manicured lawns. Neither Tracy nor I noticed anyone outside. We formed a quick hypothesis, tested it with reason and came to the same conclusion.

"Throw it out!" she shrieked, suddenly afraid that we'd be caught that second.

"I don't want to litter."

"Do it. Quick. No one's around."

Not without guilt, I tossed the bottle. Everything s.l.o.w.e.d. down in the exaggerated way of motion pictures. The bottle made a repetitive "tink" sound as it slid off of the grassy easement and tumbled along, end over end, onto the sidewalk just beyond my passenger side window. Picking up speed, the bottle finally rolled in real time to a disasterous end. As Tracy paced it with her car, we both happened to look up at the exact same time.

Standing in his yard with his elbow draped over a rake, shaking his head with a disgusted smile on his face, was Dr. Bob. Neither Tracy nor I could take our eyes off of him. Spellbound by terror.

"Oh, shit." Tracy finally blurted out.

"You can say that again."

And in that sarcastic teen-age dialogue, she did.

Come Monday morning, Dr. Bob was smugly amused about the rehearsed speech he was about to give.

"I trust everyone had a good weekend."

Everyone grumbled except Tracy and I. We murmured prayers under our breath that he would overlook us. Not a snowball's chance in Walrus's class was he ever going to offer us such grace.

"I know Lisa and Tracy had a good weekend. Did you enjoy your liquid lunch, ladies?"

He had the class's attention.

"Five star," I egged him on.

He bit into our eager class with enthusiasm. They desperately wanted to know what we'd done. To shame us into never doing it again, he continued. "You see Ms. Hopkins here decided it was a good idea to relieve herself of a beer bottle Saturday afternoon right in front of my yard." He added for dramatic sympathy, "Right after I'd just finished raking the whole thing." He told everyone that he went and picked it up and then stared at us, waiting for our counter response.

"It wasn't ours," Tracy laughed."We were just trying to get it somewhere safe."

He stared at me.

"You looked thirsty," I added.

He rolled his eyes good naturedly.

I passed Dr. Bob's class and moved on, but I never forgot the lesson he hoped I'd grasp through the veil of his sarcasm.

I will always remember Dr. Bob for his subtlety.

COLONEL SANTULLI

I magically managed to stay on the honor roll every semester in high school, despite the extensive class switching and the increasingly difficult advanced classes. The few electives I took for fun made it bearable. Along the way, I met numerous teachers, but only a few really stood out. Colonel Santulli was one of them, even though I never had him for a single class. Matt introduced us. He had him for ROTC and respected him. I knew why. Like knows like.

My mom, who spent 37 years working on Fort Leavenworth as a dedicated civilian, knew nearly all of the instructors who taught military coursework on base. She worked for the Command and General Staff College so she knew the incoming and outgoing students as well. She also made it a point to welcome the military folks who infiltrated our community, making Leavenworth their home. Of course she knew Colonel Santulli and was delighted that I'd been chosen to participate in a time- honored tradition our high school observed. Every year the students enrolled in ROTC would nominate a host of young women to represent their class. We were instructed that we should prepare a speech and present it to the class so they could vote. Only one would be crowned ROTC royalty.

I was elated to be selected in the chosen group of girls and worked diligently on my speech. In the weeks leading up to our presentations, I had more occasions to interact with the good Colonel. He already knew me well enough through Matt and by my now infamous reputation as a prankster. He always met me with smiles in the hallways and gave me a knowing look. It said, *you're up to something, I just don't know what yet, but I appreciate it.* He looked at Matt the same way, figuring we fed off of one another. I could tell he had a sense of humor about it all.

When the time came to give my speech, I was nervous, but I managed to catch Colonel Santulli's eye and something in his calm interest in what I had to say, spurred me on. I presented myself as Miss America would: with dignity, effervescent smiles and some kind words about the value of our armed forces. I probably ended with some hopeful crap about world peace. Like you do.

I didn't ultimately make the cut for the ROTC court, but I was fine with it. I was just honored to be considered.

Soon after, we had an all school pep rally in the gym. Our high school was divided into separate buildings so if you desired to cut out, between classes was the best time to do it. Jamie, Matt, another friend I'll call Kylie and I devised a strategy. None of us wanted to spend even one more hour inside when the sun beckoned us to play. Though knotted with the anticipation of skipping, half-believing we'd be caught, we forged ahead with our plan. Kylie had just gotten a different car so we elected her to be the getaway driver. Jamie would chaperone her to her car and serve as lookout. I would meet Matt at the ROTC building which was equidistant from the gym and the short bolt to the street which ran behind the high school. Matt and I would lay in wait for Kylie and Jamie to motor past and make a run for it.

When the bell rang, it was our signal. Hundreds of kids made their way to the gym. Matt and I snuck out the back entrance of the ROTC building and hid in the bushes planted on either side of the door. We were tucked into a ball, nervously shaking the bushes with our giggling and heaving. We kept readjusting our position for better camouflage, creating a storm of motion within the perfectly trimmed shrubs. Assuming he'd found two birds making out, a curious bird watcher spread the bushes apart and peered inside. We looked up to a commanding presence smiling over us. At our full height, he would've had to look up to us, but from our hunkered down position, Colonel Santulli was Goliath. Except we weren't afraid of him and had no intention of slewing him.

"So…what are you two doing down there?"

Matt was speechless. He saw his military career spiraling into oblivion, but not before considering the phone call his parents would no doubt receive.

I was considering my options and landed on clever. I leaned down and grabbed my laces. "Tying my shoes."

Colonel Santulli chuckled, "Well…if one wanted to say, skip an assembly, one should hurry up. Though one wouldn't have to worry about me, other teachers might not be as easy going."

At that moment, we saw Kylie's faint blue car pull up and stop.

Her personalized plates were a dead giveaway to the driver and a simple deduction would have revealed probable passengers.

"Thank you, Colonel Santulli!" Matt and I yelled as we sprinted toward the car.

We saw another instructor give chase and heard him yelling, "Hey!", as we dove head first into the backseat of the two-door sports car. Our noses crunched into the upholstery on impact and our feet were still sticking out the window as Kylie sped away.

The very next time I saw Colonel Santulli, he playfully put a hand over his eyes to hide them and shook his head, still laughing.

When he'd see Matt and I together on subsequent hallway passes, he grinned wide and referred to us as "well matched trouble makers." He was never serious about it. He understood we were good kids, just ornery ones. He probably understood Matt's temperament better than most. Matt came from a military family, so there was a strict code instilled in him, but he was just flippant enough not to take it all too seriously. Matt was officer material, he simply hadn't matured into the role yet.

Whereas Matt's parents fed him the necessary discipline to evolve, I was a master at bringing out his social side so no one choked him in the process.

Matt and I were soul mates. Plain and simple. We were just similar enough to maintain our friendship and just different enough to keep it interesting. We worked mowing lawns one summer. Our responsible side. We partied together. Our reckless side. We spent time studying. Our purposeful side. We went to proms together. Our romantic side. And we had a blissful knack for landing on different sides of the disciplinary scale. Our opposing side. We shared a wicked sense of humor which put all aspects into perspective.

When Matt passed away unexpectedly into young adulthood, his mom and I shared stories of his rebellious high school days.

"Do you remember when Matt got grounded for skipping out to go to lunch?" she baited.

"I don't recall." I knew every detail, but I refrained because I wanted to hear her side.

"I was driving to get food on my lunch hour when I saw our Ford Escort...that worthless old thing, always breaking down. It was sitting in the parking lot of Taco Johns. Those loud yellow Oregon plates. Couldn't miss them anywhere," she laughed reflectively. It was a memory that both amused her and ignited incredible guilt. "I was mad that he had cut class, but figuring he was just having lunch, I drove on past. An hour later, when I was driving back to work, I saw that Escort still sitting there. The car hadn't budged an inch. I was furious with him. I whipped that little Saab I drove into the parking lot and saw him casually sitting near the windows. He didn't even try to hide from me and I know he saw my car. I marched right into that restaurant, prepared to let him have it," she paused. Whisking off on a tangent as most of my fellow females do, she arced a different path in mid-story. "You know we never let him drive the Saab to take you to proms because we just couldn't trust him with it then." I knew her mother's intuition was spot-on. He didn't become a good driver until after college when he had to cough up money for his own vehicle. It changes a person. "Well, anyway, I walked into that restaurant and do you know what he says to me?"

I shook my head.

"Hi, Mom!" she laughed. "As if he didn't have a care in the world and was in no way in any trouble for ditching class."

She was enjoying the retelling. Matt was maddeningly funny. She acknowledged that he was exactly her personality. "Matt's brother is more like his dad. Matt was me when I was younger. I always appreciated his ornery streak, but his dad would get so angry. The more Larry lost it, the more Matt enjoyed himself."

Still, that day she had to play parent and so a prompt lecture fell out of her mouth. "I told Matt that he needed to finish his lunch and get back to class immediately. He would be dealt with when he got home."

I opened my mouth to further the story, but stopped myself. I wasn't sure she'd find it as hysterically funny as Matt and I did.

Matt drove home that day and found his parents angrily awaiting him. He was promptly grounded.

He called me in much better spirits than I anticipated when he opened with the news. "Mom told me that I'm not allowed to drive my car for the next two weeks. She will be driving me to and from work. And I will be walking to school."

"Well that sucks."

He was laughing hard, "Not really."

"How so?"

"Well, I know that Mom has to be up early for work, right?"

"Yes," I tried to follow the bouncing ball.

"So..." he could hardly contain himself, "I signed up for every late shift at work. I won't be getting off until midnight. By the time we wrap up, it'll be 1 in the morning. Mom has to come pick me up which I figure is about another half hour. By the time we get back home and she crawls into bed, it'll be 2 a.m. I figure she'll average a few hours of sleep every night. She'll eventually be too exhausted to continue with this punishment. I'll have my car back in no time."

"That's genius."

He was giggling, "I know."

Predictably, his mom gave up after just a few days. She was so tired that she couldn't focus at her job.

"You can drive to and from work and that's it. You're still walking to school," she told him.

Matt couldn't stop laughing when he called to share the good news. It was his first major success in evading punishment.

"The best part…" he took a moment to catch his breath, "after she told me, I dropped all of my late shifts at work and picked up earlier ones. I get off at 6 p.m. every night."

"What are you going to do until midnight?"

"I don't know. The world is my oyster. Hey, you wanna study? I think the library closes at 9."

"Of course!"

We laughed.

I bet Colonel Santulli would've appreciated it. Certainly, he would've enjoyed Matt's about face years later during his military career. I'm sure Matt didn't find the exhaustion of being awakened every few hours at basic training and having to focus on work, humorous. Not nearly as funny as his Mom would've found it, had she known what he did to her in high school. Yet I'm sure Matt still found a way to eventually laugh about it. He never truly lost his sense of humor. Perhaps that's what Colonel Santulli saw in us that sunny afternoon when we were squirreled away behind those bushes. A mirror reflection of himself.

MR. SEMPLE

If Colonel Santulli liked Matt and I, Mr. Semple treated us like family. We were pet favorites of the eccentric old teacher. He adored us. We were like the children his wife and he could never have.

Mr. Semple taught accounting at Leavenworth High School. By the time he finished with our class, all of us were majoring in the subject in college. I changed course when I had my first college level accounting class and realized, though Mr. Semple was a cool cat, the clowns I shared a classroom with at college were anything but hipsters. Boredom forced me to my advisor and the change was made to a science curriculum on the spot.

Mr. Semple was in touch with his students. He was up on the current trends and fads and kept an open, interested mind with his class. He wore sophisticated dress clothes every day with a swagger that even the most cocky athlete couldn't touch. And he was painfully funny. He understood humor and had a healthy appreciation of it.

Every year his accounting class would steal his stuffed E.T. animal. Every class would write a ransom note and leave it on his desk with a list of demands. And every year he encouraged it.

"Class, I'll have you know that every year someone steals my E.T. doll and they rue the day they tried. Let me tell you, if you even think about it, I will sniff you out and make the harshest punishment you've ever seen." Everyone in our class knew it was a dare. Maybe it was the smirk he barely hid when he threatened us. We accepted the challenge.

One day, E.T. was gone. An ominous note about his safety was on Mr. Semple's desk. I'm not saying I wrote it and I'm not saying I didn't, but let's just say, at the very least, I was brought in as a consultant.

The fun never ended in that class. Though Mr. Semple was a serious teacher and truly wanted to help us learn the material, he fostered a laid back environment that we couldn't wait to immerse ourselves in every day. Most of us anyway. And those who didn't were dismissed from his goodwill list instantaneously, never to return. He played favorites and I was one of them so I didn't pay close attention to how everyone else fared.

I noticed every nuanced detail about Mr. Semple. For instance, his best trick was asking a question during his lecture and then seeking a victim in the crowded class. He would stare in one direction and then call upon someone on the other side of the room that he fashioned either didn't know the answer or wasn't paying attention. Either way, he had a snarky insult awaiting them. He tried to maintain an expressionless face, but his give away smile always peeked through.

Evolution of a Student

Bored one Friday night, Matt and I bought chalk and drove to our school to decorate the empty campus. Matt was especially interested in harassing Mr. Semple. He raced to the teachers' smoking section where Mr. Semple loitered on his breaks, inhaling tobacco from a pipe. Matt circled the exact place where our instructor traditionally stood and wrote, "Mr. Semple's favorite spot. Hey, Mr. Semple, shouldn't you be working? Don't you have students to teach?" Underneath it he wrote, "Smoking kills, Mr. Semple, you should quit." Next to the circle, he drew a freehand stick figure smoking a pipe.

Mr. Semple magically knew who the culprit was right off. And he identified me as an accomplice.

Matt and I spent a lot of time with him after class. He was our last hour of the day and we enjoyed his company. Matt would always tell me, "Mr. Semple is my favorite teacher." He was one of mine, too.

My fondest memory of Mr. Semple was the class period where he informed us that we'd be subjected to a seating chart. Our class was sometimes a bit too chatty for the learning he hoped we'd achieve and he decided that he would periodically like to mix us up. What he failed to realize was that we were seniors, had been in almost all of our classes together and considered everyone in that class a friend. With all of my best friends in the class, Matt, Jamie and haplessly attention seeking Kylie, it would be nearly impossible to separate us enough. He placed Matt in the back and Jamie a few rows from Kylie and I. His most colossal misstep in the chart was seating Kylie directly in front of me. She was a chatterbox with everyone and though it was a smart move to place her at the front of the class, all he saw was the back of her head. She spent most of his class turned around, incessantly talking at me. Out of respect for Mr. Semple, I tried to redirect her focus to the front of the room, but Kylie was undeterred. I think that Mr. Semple realized his error in the seating chart instantly.

It was the beginning of class and he stood before us in a royal blue Pioneer spirit shirt to support our teams. He hardly ever dressed down except for game days. Beneath the t-shirt, though, everyone saw a starched oxford shirt and a tie. He was always impeccably dressed and I imagined he peeled that t-shirt off the moment he hit the parking lot and reentered the civilized world.

"Class…" he started the lecture. With Kylie still talking, he couldn't get a word in edgewise.

"Oh and did I tell you this?" Kylie rattled on.

I quietly pointed to Mr. Semple. Kylie thoughtlessly continued until she heard a stern "ahem" from the front of the room.

She turned around and I'm sure offered him a reluctant, yet charming smile which she hoped would get her off the hook.

He stared at Kylie, then me and then Kylie. When he spoke, I expected him to go after her. "Ms. Hopkins, is there a problem?"

I knew he was in more jovial spirits than the menacing look he tried to conjure up for my benefit.

To this day, I don't know what made me do it.

"Actually, I'm very glad you asked that question because there is something wrong. Terribly wrong." I launched into a skit that would've made every stand-up comedian proud, "You see, Mr. Semple, Kylie here was confused about the assignment from yesterday. But that was only because Ben gave her the wrong one. But that was only because Christina didn't know the right one. But THAT was because Matt couldn't hear you from his position in the back of the room." Occasionally, I'd vary the emphasis of the words, but the speech essentially stayed the same. "BUT that only happened because Jamie was talking to Michelle trying to understand the assignment. But that ONLY happened because Michelle copied off of Amy's paper…" I droned on and on, placing the blame on everyone in the room. At the end, it came down to me. "And that, Mr. Semple, is why no one understood the assignment and Kylie had to ask me because I was the only one paying attention." I smiled angelically.

Mr. Semple looked like he was about to burst out laughing. He kept it in and with snobbish condescension, he rolled his eyes, "Ms. Hopkins, are you quite through?"

I toyed with him a bit more. "Well, let's see…is that it?" I looked around the room to my peers who were laughing harder than I was, "Yeah, I think I'm through."

With as much mock disdain as he could muster, he asked me, "May I start class now?"

"Oh sure, don't let me stop you," I matched his sarcasm.

I could see his amused face as he shook his head and began his lecture. At the end of the class, I was packing up my books.

"Ms. Hopkins, a minute?"

Everyone filed out the door and I paused in front of him, turning to face him. Once everyone had left, he put a gentle hand on my arm. "In all my years of teaching, that is the funniest thing any student has ever done."

We broke out into a fit of laughter and maintained that space for my remaining time at LHS.

At the end of every year, Mr. Semple always chose 20 of his favorite students and invited them to his home for pizza. Matt and I drove together. Mr. Semple and his wife were incredible hosts. Their home was every bit as lovely and inviting as Matt and I imagined it would be. Expensive collections and fine art accentuated their tastefully decorated house. Once he gave us the tour, he led us onto his back patio where the table was set for us. Exercising his refined manners, he shared thoughtful stories and treated us like the adults he knew we were becoming. He had seen it all along.

Mr. Semple wrote one of my recommendation letters for college. His language let me know everything about him. He was well read and articulate. From that eloquently written letter, I learned one of my favorite words. Stellar. That's how he explained me and my intellectual achievements. I cherished his words so much that I kept that letter with me at college and pulled it out every now and then to remind me that someone besides my mom wholeheartedly believed in me.

SOMEBODY BRING HER SOME WATER

"Is that a woman or a man?" I yanked on my mom's shirt sleeve. I didn't grasp the concept as a child that my mom might be ignoring me. I just figured she didn't hear me. I projected my voice a bit louder. "MOM, is that a woman or a man?" Mom knew this was only going to get worse. She leaned in and said, "That's Missy Etheridge."

Offering me a name didn't help in my evaluation. "So is that a woman or a man?"

"It's a girl. Now shhhhh."

I was barely 8 years old and my mom had dragged me along to a high school music concert. Mom loves the performing arts, any arts really. When I was little, I didn't appreciate them as much as I do now. Back then, I was restless until something happened. Pre-show, I was all questions, embarrassing questions that only a child could ask.

I stared at this Missy Etheridge "girl" and decided she looked like my sister's date to one of the high school dances. Everyone in the '70s wore confusingly long hair in roughly similar styles.

It was difficult for me to distinguish boys from girls and Missy was no different.

Mom politely distracted my attention with misdirection. She pointed out the stage and all of the decorations. We had spent plenty of time in this theater. It used to be the only movie theater in town. I remembered being coaxed to join my mom when she wanted to see a *007* feature. It would be years before I figured out why. Mom had a crush on the suave British spy. It didn't matter who played him. I was more intrigued by the Ian Fleming books of the series, but I grew to enjoy the Bond movies just like my mom did. When the theater became a community theater, Mom was even more invested in the offerings there. I was simply enamored with the building. On the outside of it, an enormous painted circle announced that Leavenworth was the first city in Kansas. The detailed art inside the perfect sphere memorialized the city with a pictorial presentation of its history. That fascinated me.

Inside, nothing grabbed my attention and I squirmed in my seat waiting for the show to begin.

"We're here to see the Power and Life group!" my mom was excited.

"Who are they?"

"It's a chorale group that will come out and sing. The theme this year includes '50s music."

Mom loved the music of her generation and this particular performance was going to treat us to a vocal tribute ranging from the '50s to the present. The year was 1979.

The Power and Life in those days had two components, a vocal group that changed outfits nearly every number and a live band. By the time I reached Leavenworth High School, the band was replaced with a tape recording of the original songs and the vocalists wore uniforms created just for them. It wasn't nearly as much fun.

Mom was on the edge of her seat, giggling with anticipation. She couldn't wait for the show to start. I'm sure part of that was to evade the annoying series of questions her miniature companion kept asking.

"When?"

"Why?"

"How long?"

"How come?"

I had an inexhaustible supply of them.

"Oh look, they're getting ready to start," my mom clapped vigorously with the rest of the crowd hoping to drown me out. I clapped too, but I had no idea why. I wanted to ask, but the booming music filled the space and stifled me into silence.

I heard the undeniable beginning riff of "Long Train Running" by the Doobie Brothers led by a slight girl with shaggy long hair and serious guitar skills named Missy.

**

During the 1988-89 school year, I was a senior. I had friends in Power and Life and would attend their shows with my mom. Thankfully, I'm sure for her, I had no questions, only a shared enthusiasm at the prospect of being entertained. I finally understood.

I'd heard of Missy's dad at this point. Mr. Etheridge taught the class next door to my social studies class. I believe his was American Government. He was also the men's swim coach. We had never exchanged a word. I only knew him because I coveted his sky blue Mazda RX-7. Every time he drove into the parking lot, I stopped and longingly stared while he parked. It was my dream car and he owned it. I'm sure he never knew how much I loved that car. I probably should have told him.

Sitting in social studies one day, a commotion in the hallways forced our entire class to our feet. Walking down the hall toward Mr. Etheridge's classroom was a group of guys with wild '80s rock star hair being led by a smaller version of them in female form.

"Who is that?" a universal question spilled out of multiple mouths.

One student, who finally got to the window for a view, shrugged, "It's Mr. Etheridge's daughter."

"Oh," everone sighed and went back to their seats.

"We're going to see her," a few students called out and started toward the door. Our teacher forced them back inside the classroom.

Like many of my classmates, I didn't know who she was until I heard her on the radio a few months later singing her first hit, "Bring Me Some Water."

I was helping my brother wash his car in the driveway of his house when the catchy opening riff began. "Melissa Etheridge," he spoke with pride and shook his head. He went to school with her and was interested in one of her best friends back then. "She's always been a phenomenal guitar player."

My sister shared his enthusiasm. Debbie was a few years ahead of her in school, Mark a year behind. Debbie played on Melissa's softball team. "Back then she was just Missy," my sister reflected fondly.

My senior year, Melissa Etheridge treated the women's basketball champions from our school and her dad's swim team to tickets for her show and gave them backstage passes.

I kicked myself for not playing basketball in high school. The head coach Stuart Ordman, my sophomore English teacher, had tried repeatedly to talk me into it. Coach Brown, his assistant coach, was the head tennis coach and put in a great word for me and my athleticism. There were strict rules for the basketball girls and I was just craving freedom by that time. I'd confined myself too much to my academics and school sponsored extracurricular activities I participated in. I decided I needed to spend more time socializing with friends. For that, I never got the chance to play on a championship team two years running and I never got to meet Melissa Etheridge.

**

Melissa's fourth album *Yes I Am* came out as she did and my friends wanted to go. The concert venue was Leavenworth High School. My understanding was that Melissa had always dreamed of coming back to play there. She was invested in our hometown community. I liked that about her. It fit the sentimental feelings I had about where I grew up and I appreciated that she sang about our life there. I respected that she made a sizable donation to redo the theater I had sat watching her play in long ago. Her money purchased new seating and as a thank you, the city gave her some of the old ones for a keepsake. The city also earmarked a ballpark to be named in her father's memory shortly after he passed away. It made me happy that they chose to honor him. I was most excited that the city erected a sign which boasted that Melissa was from our town. She came back for the unveiling ceremony. On all occasions, I knew people who were afforded the wonderful opportunity to meet her. I would hear the stories, but it never happened for me.

I did, however, find myself attending her concert in Leavenworth and subsequent concerts over the years. The one at our high school was the best one, in my opinion. There's something about a woman willing to drag out our old marching band drums and let her whole band, including herself, perform drum solos on them, that brought back years of really good memories.

My old writing rival from second grade, Sean, was kind enough to get my ticket from that concert signed for me. Melissa was staying with his sister-in-law after the concert and he'd have access. I didn't mention that his sister-in-law was one of Mark's crushes in high school. In the way that people in small towns intersect, you were separated from knowing someone you wanted to know by one degree, not six.

**

When Melissa was diagnosed with breast cancer, a sadness befell our Leavenworth community and the Chamber of Commerce rallied behind her for support. I had been living in Kansas City for awhile and wasn't aware of my hometown's efforts. My mom called to tell me the news.

"The chamber purchased a card for the residents and former residents to sign. They're going to send it to her."

"Are you going to sign it?" I asked her.

"I already did." I could hear the concern in her voice.

I found out the details and together with my friend Andy, we drove the forty miles just to sign the card. When I arrived, a soft spoken woman, who took her role in the gesture very seriously, told us the requisite information and asked for proof of our connection to Leavenworth. I told her I graduated from Leavenworth High School and explained that Melissa's dad taught at the school when I attended there. I further explained my connections through my siblings.

The woman was apologetic, "I'm sorry I have to ask all of these questions. We've had some unwelcome visitors from a church that doesn't support her lifestyle and have made their presence known. They're just very hateful. So we're being cautious."

I knew exactly of which church she spoke. "I'm sorry you have had to endure that. There's certainly nothing Godly in their actions. I support Melissa."

She smiled and began sharing about the time Melissa came to town and did a documentary on the city and her hometown roots. The woman was engaging and pleasant and grateful that we were lending our support. She handed us the oversized card.

Andy knew what he wanted to say right off and signed the card promptly. I had to contemplate my words carefully. I wanted to save room for the other people who wished to sign and yet convey my heartfelt empathy for Melissa's road ahead. I prayed upon my words and finally put pen to paper. What I wrote was intentional and spiritual. I focused not just on her physical healing, but on healing all levels: her emotions, mind and spirit. The words came by grace and I wrote them with purpose. I trusted the words because they were created from the deepest part of my spirit. They came through me, but they weren't mine to own.

I was surprised that I received a voicemail message from one of my Kansas City friends hours later.

"Hey, I loved what you wrote Melissa Etheridge. Very powerful words, my friend."

I had no idea what he was talking about. I hadn't made the connection.

When I called him, he told me that the local news had picked up the story of what Leavenworth was trying to do in support of one of our own. They focused the camera on the card and highlighted my sentiments. My words of thoughtful encouragement were there for the viewing of the entire Kansas City metro area. I smiled and hoped those words offered support to everyone diagnosed with cancer.

Melissa overcame her health issue and for that, a wide-sweeping relief spread throughout the Leavenworth community and beyond.

I will remember Melissa Etheridge for the rest of my life. Not just because of her music which I've found deep meaning and resonance with over the years. I've always said, there's something special about standing in the same locations as another person and feeling the same exact things, knowing their words speak for you. I will remember her not for the memories shared through others in their connection with her. Not from knowing her musical abilities before the world did and being afforded the opportunity to enjoy them. It's not even because we graduated from the same high school and will forever be Leavenworth Pioneers. And it's surprisingly not because she beat breast cancer and belted out that hair raising rendition of "Piece of My Heart" at the Grammy's that year, boldly walking on stage, bald, so you could see the face of cancer. No, it's none of these soul stirring memories that will forever captivate my attention. The reason I will remember Melissa Etheridge is because her dad drove that sky blue little

Mazda RX-7 that I pined for and wished I'd driven, back when life was simple and you had, in her words, "no place to go." It's a symbol linked to a memory of youth and all the dreams I dreamed under the same mid-west sky as she did once upon a long ago. It represents the courage to make my most profound dreams come true. Just like she did. That's why I will always remember Missy.

MS. PIC

I signed up for the class because it was an English credit and I had decided to use all of my electives to pursue my passion for the subject my senior year. This class was rumored to be an easy A. No one who had completed the class could tell me anything more than this because the class surpassed understanding in its scope and meaning. It wasn't blatantly titled like other classes. There was no reference to its subject matter and no faceless numbers following it. It would've been an injustice to call it English 101 or other such cold titles. It was simply called Quest.

Ms. Pic, our instructor, stood humbly in front of our class. Her hands were clasped in front of her prayerfully. She gazed around our room with a serene smile on her face, a sort of reverence for the students who chose to spend time with her for the semester. It was the first elective for me that would only last one semester. Its brevity made me think it might be a fluff class. I'd soon learn it was anything, but that.

"Good morning, class. Welcome to Quest. My name is Pic Thompson, but you can call me Ms. Pic."

The rambunctious students quelled into a calm I'd not seen in any classes prior to this one. I believe it was because of the soothing energy of our class leader, who stood respectfully before us.

Ms. Pic was in her 60's. Her hair was graying and she didn't try to hide the fact. I appreciated her decision. It was honest. She maintained a solitary spit curl and wore horn rimmed glasses, throwbacks to a generation gone by. Dresses were her staple and she wore them modestly. Overall, she looked like the Church Lady from Saturday Night Live and I found it charming.

I took stock of our class. We were quite the misfit bunch. Honor students, wallflowers, athletes, druggies, you name the stereotype and it was represented.

"This class is an English credit, but we will be doing far more than grammar, paperwork and required readings in this class. Everyone begins this class with an A. So long as you complete the required work, I intend to give you one."

I saw kids who hadn't seen an A throughout their entire education sigh with relief. They were the most excited for this class and hung on her every word. Oh how their parents would love that surprise when report cards were released.

"Now you've gone and done it, Junior. With all of your pot smoking and underachieving, I bet you'd never get an A. I hope you've saved your allowance. Someone has to pay off my bookie!"

I saw those kids flicker with the same imagined conversation. Still, you couldn't wipe the pride off of their faces. An A. Who would ever expect that? And the answer was a resounding, no one.

Ms. Pic had an assistant teacher who followed her dutifully and handled us just as lovingly as Pic did. Not in all my school years had any teacher ever had a personal assistant. It was a most mesmerizing learning environment.

The coursework was divided into sections which spoke directly to the most common emotions people experienced: Love, Respect, Fear, Anger, Joy and a range of other emotions. And Ms. Pic was the perfect teacher to open these sensitive discussions because she never judged us.

"On occasion, class, I will ask you for a copy of your work. If you wish to share, please do. I keep them. I treasure them. I assure you that I never throw them away when I've asked you for it. The share, however, is up to you. I will never force you to do it."

When she would require we journal as part of the class, either on topic or in whatever subject we felt needed private discussion, she would begin with, "I will be asking you to journal your feelings today. There is no length requirement and you may use whatever language you choose to express yourself. I will never ask you to share this and when I walk by, I will only be checking to be sure you've completed the task. I will never read your journals. They are for you." True to her word, she looked over our shoulders and sometimes placed a loving hand upon them, but she never hovered.

She respected us. She was a religious woman who understood the unconditional love of her faith. She proudly displayed her cross necklace, but she never preached to us. She embraced us.

"I would never expect you to share your life with me, if I didn't share mine with you," she began class one day. "I am an amateur radio enthusiast. My husband works for the Red Cross. You might see him around town. His name is Bill and he's easily approachable. Don't hesitate to say "hi" and introduce yourself if you see him. He loves meeting my students. I'm also an amateur braillist. I am currently translating some beloved literary classics to braille for the blind people I work with."

Ms. Pic spoke right to the soul of everyone in that room. When she shared herself, we found even more reason to love her. Initially, we loved her because she so obviously loved us.

With every short story, poem and journal entry we penned, we learned grammar. With every story we read, we plumbed our emotions and revealed our critical thinking skills. It was a class, but if felt more like a self-help seminar.

I remember the day Ms. Pic had us a read a poem entitled "I'm Not Okay, You're Not Okay and That's Okay." It was a favorite of hers. In turn, all of us had to share our favorite one. Mine was a Robert Frost poem I've loved since fifth grade, "Fire and Ice." I also loved his more popular, "The Road Not Taken." If you asked me now, I'd say it's "Blight" by Ralph Waldo Emerson, but back then I was all about Mr. Frost. One student shared a bitter essay by Jenny Holzer with a line ending, "Do you want to fall not ever knowing who took you?"

Ms. Pic never batted an eye. Everyone was entitled to feel and express themselves in the way they needed to.

When we did our exercises, the true learning of the class took place. The questionnaire we filled out titled, "How Well Do I Know My Parents?", took me by surprise. I thought I knew everything there was to know about my 'rents, but when I had my parents fill out the exact same questionnaire, their answers differed more than anticipated. I learned that even when we love someone, there's always so much more to know. It always pays to ask periodically. Things change and people do, too.

The day after I handed in another assignment, where we were to write about someone we admired, Ms. Pic pulled me aside. "I notice that you wrote about Debbie Lauxman. Lisa, I think you should send her a copy of this letter."

I was silent. I wasn't prepared for that request.

Sensing my hesitance, she made a heartfelt offering, "You know when you feel positive things about people, you should tell them. You never know how much they may need to hear what you have to say. How much it may mean to them."

I agreed.

When Ms. Pic paired us with students we hardly spoke to in the hallways, we learned that people are rarely ever what they seem. It's true I spoke to everyone no matter what because it was how my parents raised me, but I discovered that I had underestimated a few classmates and that didn't feel right inside. I adjusted my thinking, especially after Johnny's share one morning.

Johnny was an outcast in every sense, but the morning Ms. Pic asked him to share his poem with the class, he nervously stood and let loose with tear worthy iambic pantameters that left us all speechless. Nothing so beautiful had streamed from anyone's lips in that room and he spoke it with a grace that not one person expected.

When Ms. Pic had us do self-esteem building exercises and charts that evaluated our friendships, it was revelatory. Seeing my best friends' behaviors written alongside my own in my own handwriting, it became clear who should remain in my circle of influence and who probably needed to be released.

"Today, class, we're going to pair up," Ms. Pic opened one day. "We are going to disagree on paper. One person will start by writing a statement. The other will refute it and pass it back. This exercise will continue until I call time."

I was paired with my friend Cary. We were both of the same waggish temperament so I was especially excited to try my hand at besting her in this exercise. I wrote out, "Cary, I just want you to know how sorry I am that I slept with your boyfriend."

It was an obvious false statement because Cary didn't have a boyfriend at the time and I would never do such a thing, but it left the field wide open for our debate. I handed the paper off to Cary and waited while she took her time writing a response.

When Ms. Pic called "switch", Cary handed it back. "Lisa, I

know you thought you were so clever and got away with it, but the truth is, I knew. I was going to tell you that he had an STD, but you never asked and I figured that you'd find out sooner or later. And anyway, no hard feelings because I slept with yours, too. You're right, he was a great lay."

I was choking back laughter as I responded, "Gee, Cary, I'd say you were a bitch for doing that, but all things considered, it would be an injustice. Your boyfriend told me that he lied about the STD because he didn't really enjoy having sex with you and preferred to hold out for something better. Guess I'm it. And as for my boyfriend, well, can I really call him that? I wonder since he's saving money for that sex change and all. I admit that your confession does make me question your devotion to our friendship." Ms. Pic spoke a quiet "switch." I handed the paper back to Cary. I watched her read it and the tears swell in her eyes, she was laughing so hard I worried I might have to administer CPR. She thought for awhile and finally put the pen to paper just seconds before Ms. Pic called "switch" a final time.

I read Cary's final lines, though it was difficult to focus over Cary's laughter. It simply read, "Lisa, I'm so sorry you feel that we had a friendship. I hate to say this, since you've been so kind over the years, but the truth is, I never liked you."

We were laughing so hard by the time the bell rang that we didn't even notice class was over.

I still remember Cary sharing her favorite song in small group exercises a week later, "Here I Go Again." It was part of a larger project for the class that required we choose our favorite song and make a visual aid that spoke to our reasons for selecting it.

My mom helped me create a scene from the banks of the Missouri River using plywood as a base, sand from a local concrete company, fake water I created out of paper and a bridge Mom and built using toothpicks. I painted it red, but the Centennial Bridge was more bland than that. Mom dug out some tinsel from a Christmas storage box and I spray painted it green for shrubbery. It was a challenge to haul that entire project to class. By the time I played the song, "Watching the River Run" by Loggins and Messina, I had the attention of my small group. I explained that I'd been suicidal my sophomore year and spent three months alone at this particular spot, fighting for a reason to live. It was over a love connection gone terribly wrong. I didn't elaborate and my peers didn't press the issue. I think my classmates were more stricken that a popular girl, who always wore a smile on her face, had ever considered ending such a beautiful life. Still, we were at a place in this class where every share was respected and no one made adverse commentary. They listened. They supported. And when I told them I found God in those moments, they understood. I played the song and everyone just listened. I also played "I'm Alright" by Loggins at another point in class. It was understood that whatever affliction I suffered, I was over it.

One day we walked into class and Ms. Pic informed us that we would be entertaining some very special guests that morning. "A few female inmates from the Kansas Correctional Facility in Lansing will be coming in to speak to you, class. Ask any questions you like."

One student already knew what question he wanted to ask, but he had to be sure. "Anything?"

Ms. Pic nodded solemnly. "Anything."

When the women entered, we were all on our guard. They were not chained, but entered wearing orange jumpers and sat down in front of the classroom. A guard I recognized from somewhere sat nearby and smiled at our class.

The women all opened by introducing themselves and telling us about their crimes. Hard to believe that they were behind bars because all of them were innocent, or so they said.

When the Q & A began, the enthusiastic question asker's hand shot up. One of the women nodded towards him.

"I was wondering, do you have sex with each other while you're in prison?"

Our classmates groaned, but it was a legitimate question. One he'd apparently heard somewhere and needed confirmation of it.

"No, we're not allowed to do that," they answered and smiled at one another like they were eyeing a dessert tray.

"We do get conjugal visits," the outspoken one of the group answered for them.

No one bothered to inquire what that meant.

"Do you get to wear makeup or do your hair with a curling iron or anything like that?" a girly girl asked, nearly dreading the thought of being without her beauty accessories.

"No makeup, but we do get appliances," the outspoken one again. "We're in minimum security so we can have up to two appliances at a time. We can periodically trade the ones we have for others. So one day we might have a toaster and then exchange it for a blow dryer. It works like that," she answered. She was the one, I remembered, who had murdered an old man. She said that he wanted to die because he was sick and she'd helped him do it. There was no directive anywhere so stating his wishes and even if there was, she would have a difficult time with that defense. All things considered, when you're not even in health care, it's a tough sell. And nowadays, even if you are a health professional, you're doing time. Ask Dr. Kavorkian.

When they finished answering questions, the outspoken humanitarian told us that we should consider ourselves lucky. "Stay in school. Do the right things. You don't want to end up like us."

What? Innocent?

I understood what Ms. Pic was trying to do. She taught us not to judge other members of society. They are people and deserve respect just like we do.

By the time I walked out of that class with my A, I felt like I'd been altered into someone new. The class taught us how to be human beings. I saved every note I had in that class. Years would prove it was the only class I felt compelled to do so.

**

I saw Ms. Pic one last time when I was visiting home during my freshman year of college. I was driving along one sunny afternoon when I saw her gardening in her yard. I pulled over and said hello.

"How's school going, Lisa?"

"Not as well as I expected. It's much tougher on the college level. I was used to getting mostly A's the whole way through high school and I've had to swallow B's and even a few C's in college."

"You're a good student. Don't let that discourage you at all. College is tough. You will do fine. You will graduate and make all of us so proud. It was such a joy to educate you."

I beamed, "Yours was one of my favorite classes. I saved all of your notes."

"And I saved all of yours," she smiled back.

We spoke of a good friend's death and I told her it affected my studying habits because it's all I thought about. Ms. Pic was genuinely empathetic.

"I understand how you're feeling, Lisa, but life does go on. We have to have faith." She stared into my eyes and I could tell that the advice was more personal for her. "I admit my own struggles recently," she paused, reflective, "I have cancer."

"Oh no," I blurted out. I imagine that didn't make her feel any better, but I was so saddened by the news.

We finished a very touching conversation and parted ways.

"Stop back by and see me," she said. It was the last thing she ever said to me.

I had planned to drive back home specifically to see Ms. Pic the following semester. I had some good news to share on the academic front. She died a few weeks before I had scheduled to come home.

I miss her, but the truth of her lessons lives always in my heart. She's on her own Quest now. I'm so grateful for what she taught me and more importantly, the way she taught me. I'll never forget her.

OSHITOGRAPHY

My first year at university was a liberating and exhausting pursuit of forming my personality in my new environment. It was tough to make connections with professors at this level considering the sheer size of the classroom environment and the theater seating which was not conducive to personal interaction with nearly anyone. I hardly knew the people in my classes and I lived off campus my first year which I now know is a tragic mistake. I learned, though, possibly more about life and how to juggle it than I did in my formative educational years. With Mom not around to have dinner prepared and no dining halls, I was forced to make do with the skills I'd learned in the token cooking class I enrolled in my senior year of high school. I wished I had time to create those elaborate dishes, but I wound up with a heavily stocked cabinet of Kraft macaroni & cheese that first year. To this day, I can barely choke down one bite of the sinister orange paste.

Parking at the university was a nightmare I also endured that first year. I lived just far enough away to have to drive, and nearly every day I would get duped by a lady I called the Parking Lot Troll. Every morning she would sit in one of a fleet of vehicles she owned. Motor running. Exhaust belching fumes. Her tail lights would occasionally come on and I would get excited because she always had the best spot. Inevitably, after ten or fifteen minutes of idling with my blinker on, she would shut the car off and get out, launch her backpack over her shoulder, and scurry to class, smirking the whole way. It was a game she played and I hated it. I'm unsure how I never seemed to recognize her. Perhaps it was her clever disguises or her ever changing vehicles. I don't know if she owned a car lot or what, but some days it was a minivan, others a hoopty, occasionally a new car. I fell for her tricks for almost an entire semester. It was not until I played her little game on her one day that I realized how much fun she was having and periodically chose to introduce her game to other frustrated drivers.

By the time I would make it to my class, I was winded from the arduous journey, even for being in shape at the time. I rarely found my classes stimulating enough to be worth my extensive travels to get there. I didn't have any favorite professors that first year. I can only say I had memorable ones and not always for the best reasons.

I met Mr. Smith, the husband of my future anatomy instructor, my first semester. Mrs. Smith was an educational tyrant whom I came to adore, whereas I found her husband a rather dull counterpart. Mr. Smith's class was a required freshman biology course. Only, he didn't really teach the class. Our lectures were pre-recorded on tapes and we had to come in to the labs during the week and take notes from his monotone recordings. He only showed up on actual lab days. I found the coldness of the learning environment a challenge at first. It took a fellow student sharing the gift of making note cards to study from that spared my grade in the lecture portion. The labs were nothing to write home about, either. Mr. Smith took us outside to bird watch one day and explained how avian sex identification was tremendously difficult. It didn't keep him from trying. Bird anatomy. Really?

In later years, I would lose my beloved bird because she had a sex specific disease and I didn't know her gender at the time. It was too difficult to tell.

I wished then that I had paid more attention in Mr. Smith's lab class. I tried, but it was a snoozer class and I wasn't the only one napping. Periodically, we'd catch Mr. Smith nodding off in mid-sentence. Hell, if the professor can't stay awake during his own class, what was my inspiration to do so?

I would come to find out that Mr. Smith had a condition known as narcolepsy. It explained a lot when I finally took the time and interest to explore what this actually meant. I passed his class, thankfully, because I sure didn't want to retake it. And in the end, Mr. Smith indirectly got me my first real job post-graduation. My own withered experiences in his class inspired me to form a snarky outgoing voicemail message.

"You have reached the narcoleptic suicide hotline. Please leave your message at the ...zzzzzzzzzzzzzzzzzzzzzzzzzzzzzzzz."

I had forgotten to change the greeting when I applied for a job with HealthSouth, a physical rehabilitation facility. The head administrator called me straight away to set up an interview. When she mentioned the message in passing, I just knew she would scrutinize me and my ability to render compassionate care to her patients.

Instead, she completed our interview, looked me in the eyes and said, "I have to admit that the reason I called you was because of the outgoing voicemail message on your phone."

Oh shit. Here it comes.

"That's the funniest thing I've ever heard. I called you on the spot. You have a great sense of humor and you'll need one for this job."

I wish she was kidding.

The night three different nurses overlooked a patient's chart, each administering a variant form of laxative to the patient, I walked into a nightmare straight out of my anatomy lab experiences. I had to move on from that position. I was on my way to being a physical therapist at the time and secretly glad I'd opted out of nursing as a career choice.

No other instructors my freshman year besides Mr. Smith had that sort of marionette ability to get me a future job. My modern dance instructor sure didn't. He was a flaming twit. His being gay was not an issue for me. His being an idiot, however…

I had an A in his class when I got desperately sick in the last month of my second semester. I had to go home. Mononucleosis, which ran rather rampant on our campus that year, weakened my immune system and I contracted chicken pox. I was exhausted and couldn't do even one more plie. He was anything, but sympathetic.

I had enrolled in the class to learn to dance like Janet Jackson, but quickly discovered that "modern" dance didn't mean "current."

"Express yourself with movement. Let your body carry your emotional message," the tights wearing miniature Baryshnikov would squeal. I loved to dance and did understand the gist of his instructions, but I would've rather shoveled horse shit from a local stable than sit through his class. The fact remained, though, I had an A when my illness forced me to have to leave the university temporarily. When I came back that summer to take my finals, he informed me that I would not be offered one in his class. I would have to either take a C or retake the entire class.

"How is that fair?" I asked him.

"Well, this is an experiential class. You weren't here to experience it. You missed a month of class." He failed to consider that it was only 4 classes.

"I experienced enough."

When he refused to negotiate, I took the C and moved on. No way in hell I was flying through the air on the wings of my limbic system for one more semester.

The professor who was most empathetic to my illness, and willing to issue me a final the instant I asked for one, was a Jacques Cousteau looking fellow from Western Kansas who fashioned himself a seafarer. He taught Oceanography 101. I joked that I took the class to learn prime locations for spring break, but I knew it was a science class.

Loving the ocean sight unseen, I wanted to learn about her before my first encounter with her. I figured a few lectures on the pull of tides and the influence of weather would be included in the curriculum. And then a dreamy dissertation on how many islands he'd visited and hopefully, the local hot spots. Not even close. I learned about the pull of the tides, true, and how to swim back into shore when caught in a rip tide. The class, though, was heavily weighted in chemistry, biology and a dash of physics. I cried nearly every test. I've had some extremely challenging classes throughout my academic career, but none as difficult as Oshitography.

The professor's tests were surreal. Ten questions. Multiple choice. That's it. At first, I found myself excited for the brevity of it. Then he explained that each question was worth 10 points for a total of 100 points. He failed to say that the questions were each a page long which included multiple choice answers that equated to paragraphs. If you merely guessed an answer and got it right, good for you, an easy 10 points. But if you got it wrong, you automatically lost 10 points. What he expected his students to do was evaluate which parts of each multiple choice answer were correct and note it with a T for true. Also noting which statements were false and denoting it with an F. In this way, we were to reason which answer was most true. If we played by his rules, even if we got the answer wrong, he would give us partial credit. It was a daunting proposition.

I did well in the class, until the third test where I got a C. I didn't find myself hiding in bathrooms as I did when I received my very first C on a test. I considered myself lucky. Especially when I looked around to the other casualties of the class who got hooked on one of his trick lines. What got to me about the grade was the note he scribbled on the top of my paper. "You can do better." He noticed his students in a class of hundreds. He took the time. I respected that about him.

I was pulling a low B in the class at the time I got sick. When I came back to take the final, I knew I didn't score well. Too much time away from the material and in that class, unlike modern dance, it was not something you could make up with a spin or a twist, no matter how much emotion I put into it. I failed my first class. I was crushed. The final was so heavily weighted that a low mark bottomed out your grade. I knew I could do better.

I enrolled in the class again the following semester for my own peace of mind. I had a younger instructor who was not nearly as enamored with the subject matter as old Jacques. When the final grade came out the second time, I had lost the "B" I had averaged the entire semester. I wound up with a C. C for a class on seas. It was poetic.

ANOMALY

The first time I heard the word anomaly was in my anatomy class at Kansas State University. It's also the first time I heard the phrases: "Oh wow, a bucket of penises!" and "Her pubis is preserved in formaldehyde." Though my all time favorite sentiments and the ones that would linger with me equally as long as the stench of the cadaver preservatives in my nostrils and clothes was, "Dead bodies will make you hungry. You don't think so now, but soon you'll be craving a Snickers bar." I thought the guy was kidding. When he didn't crack a smile, I worried.

Anatomy and Physiology, A&P to those in the know, is the cornerstone class of all health care related academic pursuits. At Kansas State, it was a 6 credit hour class which roughly translated to a plummeting GPA if you failed it. I noted the academic force of the class and offset it with classes the equivalent of riflery and bowling. Why risk it?

The first day I walked into class, the matronly A&P professor stared at us through thick bifocals and scared us into submission. "This class is the hardest class you will take on this campus, I assure you." She gave us anything, but a welcome to the class. She rather dared us to fail it by not committing our souls to her for the semester. "You will need to spend every spare moment in the lab studying, if you expect to pass." To add further terror, she informed us that she was writing the textbook for next semester's class, just in case we failed to heed her warning and wound up taking it again. She listed the drop dates for the course and glanced around the room, noting who she could count on to fail out early so she could adequately place her bets in the office pool.

She proceeded to give us her review of the inferior textbook we'd be using until her scholarly upgrade hit the shelves. "Not to worry, I will ensure that this course is supplemented with my loose leaf versions."

Glad I wasted seventy bucks on the piece of outdated shit before me, I thought. Wonder what the resale value would be at Varney's Bookstore at the end of the semester. It probably wouldn't be enough to buy a beer. You could always judge a good textbook by how many beers it bought you on book buy back day. Thank God for dollar pitcher night or I'd have disliked my instructor more than I fashioned I did already.

We were told to pick our lab partners that day. I looked around trying to find the oldest students I could. They tended to make the best lab partners because they had already majored in Life with an emphasis in Fuck Off and had settled down. I really wanted to hunker down, focus and pass the class the first time and I knew my lab partners were the key to my success. I made a casual pass of the pensive faces surrounding me. I noticed the homely woman in her thirties with goggles for glasses and the hot young newlywed in her late twenties who had already failed the class once. Perfect. The homely lady would surely be home studying every night and the newlywed would have the old tests to study off of. It was a genius plan.

I turned on the charm that first class and by the end, I'd partnered with my coveted two choices. The older woman had already pre-read the textbook. She made a great first impression. The other girl was a reformed slacker and I knew she was focused for the semester.

I made some anatomical posters that first day and hung them on my apartment's kitchen wall with push pins the size of railroad ties that spelled, deposit return questionable. I referred to those posters every day because anatomy lingo and the anatomical locations were foreign to me and I kept forgetting the things I'd just read. I made note cards to improve my memory and placed my hat in the ring as a lab partner to be reckoned with, for certain.

The first thing that hit me in anatomy lab was that infamous smell. Formaldehyde is an undeniable stench that clings to your clothing and seeps into your very pores. There was no denying the fact that I was in anatomy class. Everywhere I walked on campus, people would cross a path to avoid me. Elevator encounters were equally as polarizing. People tried to hide their gagging by pulling their shirts over their noses. It was a badge of pride for the anatomy students. For even though we wreaked in a way that denied sexiness, students still admired those they deemed academically superior and being in A&P certainly bolstered that campus cred.

Our instructor, Mrs. Smith, was a phenomenal educator in a

one-on-one setting, but in class she mocked us as if her very IQ lowered when she was in our presence. She was pompous, but she knew anatomy like the back of her vein laden, artery infused hands. The first day that lab class officially began, she introduced us to her trusty assistant. He was in his forties, a thin, wiry guy who looked like he hadn't seen the sun since birth. He was kind and helpful, though, and that made up for most of what he lacked in physical attractiveness. Plus, he graded a lot of our papers and that gave him downright sex appeal, at least for the semester.

After learning our way around the basic components of the lab, we were led into the room with the cadavers. A perky, suck ass student assistant introduced us to the newly departed who donated themselves so generously for us to learn. The assistant then enlisted several chiseled male students to pull five gallon paint drums from the sturdy metal shelves hanging around the room. The muscle heads, who initially were gung ho to volunteer for the task, grimaced when they reached for their respective buckets. They sagged under the weight of the purportedly fluid filled plastic containers, making their countless hours at the gym seem like a sincere waste of time. Maybe they should have tried yoga or better yet, slacked off with beer and pizza like the rest of us and left the heavy lifting to the candy asses who frequented the gym on a more regular basis. Bet they wouldn't try that overachieving shit again.

I hung back with my lab partners, waiting expectantly to find out what was in said containers. When the student assistant ripped the lids off, we were stunned to see buckets of individual body parts soaking in formaldehyde.

"Oh wow, a bucket of penises!" I heard one student exclaim.

Students gathered around plunging for body parts, but by far the most impressive catch were the penises. They enthralled everyone. Hearts, brains and a few livers were interesting, too, but the only body part that rivaled the penis was a female pubis that had basted in formaldehyde sauce for three decades.

"Her pubis has been preserved in formaldehyde!" Our student assistant announced proudly.

She handed each of us a special pair of forceps to splay the labia apart. For the young nerds who'd never seen a vagina up close, the study was better than porn. Everyone was respectful enough not to comment, however. Even the young girls who studied the penises and were carefully considering the accuracy of the six inch measurement they'd been given by their boyfriends.

I was struck by how the whole scene was remarkably similar to bobbing for apples.

When I saw the cowboy who told me I'd be famished when I started working on the cadavers, I avoided him. I considered him a creeper of which I wanted no part. After the first few weeks, however, I found myself sharing a Snickers with him in the lounge, the delightful scent of formaldehyde creating a pleasant aromatherapy between us. Ah, ambiance.

The first test was brutal. We had two minutes on the clock at each station our instructor had set up. There were boxes lying side by side in a line on the last row of tables with bones hidden inside. By feel, we had to determine the bone's name and scribble it on our test papers in the allotted time. The cadavers, skin peeled back by the dissection team, had pins stuck in random organs and vessels making the scene look more like an acupuncture treatment than a testing environment. Slides shoved under microscopes made for kaleidoscope images of cell tissue for our identification. The visual display was both fascinating and mind boggling at the same time. Large skeletons with stickers shoved into various orifices and hanging off of random structures, made me wish I'd studied even harder than I already had.

After that miserable first test in which I scored a passing grade, but not nearly what I wanted, our instructor offered extra credit.

"I would like for you to create a new organ. It can be anything you want. I ask that you draw a picture of your creation. Tell me where it's located in the body and give me the details of its function, blood supply and which organs it may or may not attach to."

I thought about it for weeks. Many pots of coffee, packets of No Doz and gallons of soda later, I created the lipogus. I attached it straight from the esophagus directly to the large intestine with a relatively clean shot out of the asshole, though I'm sure I said anus in my paper. The lipogus was ingenius. It filtered out saturated fat in foods and promptly eliminated the waste in the stool. I drew it as a tube which connected to the esophagus. It swelled into a balloon at its halfway point, nestling behind the stomach like a shadowed stalker. The tail of it was also tubular in nature and sat behind the intestines with a tie in at the descending colon. The saturated fat would pass through the lipogus, entering the descending colon before traveling through the sigmoid colon and rectum and finally exiting via the anus. I turned my paper in, very proud of my work. I received an A because my instructor was so in love with the idea. I was ahead of the newlywed's test scores with that extra credit, though homely lady was the odds on favorite to win best grade in the class.

The day that stands out was the day we were to investigate the small and large intestines on the cadavers and take our requisite notes. My lab partners and I stayed late. In the final hour the building was open, we were the only three who remained in the lab. We worked quickly and with utter dedication. Like fine oiled machines, as they say, we took notes in turn and scarcely overlapped the information we gleaned important. Copies of our individual notes would be made and shared among our little group for studying purposes.

I was delirious from lack of sleep and playful in the lab that evening. Gloved and curious, I noted the lily pad shapes of the fatty cells resting in a liquefied stew near the cadaver's basin just below the lower bowel. Our straight A, older lab partner had gently shoved the many feet of intestines out of the way. It made the adipose cells readily visible and far too appealing not to have a feel. I dipped my hands in the fluid, immersing them, and in a few quick swipes, splashed the formaldehyde around just a bit. When one of my index fingers got stuck in something soft and gooey, I hesitantly removed it. On my finger was a dollop of shit. Inadvertently, I had found the lowest portion of the large intestine which had been sliced vertically in order to reveal the tissue inside.

The newlywed cupped her hand over her mouth and managed to mutter, "I think I'm going to be sick," before she sprinted out of the room.

I was still staring at my finger, horrified.

My older lab partner adjusted her glasses and looked at me. Without fanfare, she stated matter-of-fact, "It's feces. When they preserve the bodies, they typically are not able to remove all of it from the bowel." Then she put her head down and kept writing notes.

I glanced over to my Snickers bar, resting quietly on the dissection table and discovered that it really didn't satisfy in that moment. Same with my soft drink. I tossed them in the trash and discarded my gloves into the hazardous waste container on my way out of the lab.

I felt like an anomaly amongst my peers, the one who deviates from the norm. I didn't see anyone else in class playing with poo.

I passed the class and moved along my academic highway, but I kept the outdated textbook to remind me that I had a lot left to learn.

IT'S BETTER THAN SEX!

I've always been afraid of heights. Even for all of my flustered attempts to work on ladders during my summer painting excursions with my brother, I never got over it.

Perhaps it's because he terrorized me from the ground level, rocking the ladder as I clung for dear life, shakily holding a bucket of paint with both arms wrapped around the metal stairs.

"It's the wind!" he'd call out laughing.

I never bothered to look down. I knew he was the culprit.

The day the wind actually did kick up a gust while I gripped the ladder with white knuckles from three stories high, Mark did the unthinkable. Considering my panicked position atop the ladder trying to paint a soffit and knowing I was trapped, he used the strong tornado-like wind swaying my foundation to his advantage. He stealthily climbed up behind me. I didn't notice. The wind had swayed the ladder for the better part of an hour, any extra shifting only made my prayers more fervent and my grip even tighter. Looking around would've only made me more petrified. When he reached the few rungs below me, Mark brushed his fingers against my calves and made a gentle buzzing noise. If I was afraid of heights, I was equally terrified of wasps. It was hell. I screeched and suddenly it occurred to Mark that we could both go tumbling down. Dummy.

"What were you thinking?" I screamed.

He was beyond laughter, into hysterics, "Calm down. If you move, we're both done for."

I slathered my brush with paint and canvassed his arm. He only wiped it back on me, but it was a move that I hoped would deter any further harassment.

"I'll quit," I threatened.

"No, you won't," he laughed. "You know you wouldn't have nearly as much fun on any other job as you do with me."

True, but that day had me ruminating the possibilities.

"It's no wonder I have a fear of heights!" I yelled at him as he descended the ladder.

Perhaps that's why he showed up that blustering day I chose to jump out of the proverbial, perfectly good airplane. He had been calling me at college for weeks, playing Lyle Lovett's song, "Since the Last Time." If he wasn't playing it for me, he was singing the line, "I went to a funeral…"

No one, but my parents believed I was serious about jumping.

My former dorm buddies, Jared and Ben, had joined a few other guys for a skydiving experience in a town called Wamego, a half hour from our university. They came back wide-eyed and pumped plumb full of adrenaline.

Jared confessed in private that he'd likely never do it again, but it was worth it. Ben told me he loved it, but having some problems with his risers made him reconsider a second attempt. The risers are connecting straps that contain the lines which run from the parachute to the container. The container is like a backpack that initially houses the parachute and another reserve chute. No wonder he was shaken by the whole incident. So many safety factors depended on those risers and the resultant lines being straight.

They urged me to give it a try. I weighed it out carefully and decided that I would ultimately like to do it.

"Maybe it will help me face my fear of heights," I was optimistic.

That summer, I stayed on campus taking a class. I worked for the Athletic Department painting the football stadium with the student athletes who were on work study. I saved every penny I could. When the summer job ended, my boss offered to keep me on to work as the Supervisor of Operations for the newly built press box. I would be working the football games and get admission for free. What broke college student wouldn't do that? Once the season was complete, he offered me the chance to stay on with the Athletic Department and tutor athletes. It was a gift. I had more than enough money to skydive.

I signed up for the class and talked my friend Phil into joining me. Phil. He took some convincing, but eventually agreed because he felt like he owed me one.

**

Phil started college unable to communicate with people in a social setting. When I met him, he couldn't look anyone in the eyes and only spoke in terms of baseball. When I finally figured out how to command his attention, it had been months. I would sit with him in the student entertainment room in the basement of our dorms, watching his beloved St. Louis Cardinals play.

"The Royals are better," I would rib him.

He would spend a lot of time explaining the error in my thinking. I would retaliate with a discussion of uniform colors, blue being far superior to red. I told him I picked teams according to the colors of their jerseys. It was true when I was a kid, but I'd evolved since then. I knew the sport inside out. I chose to joke with him anyway. I was trying to lighten his load. He didn't understand humor. He hadn't laughed in years.

We would sit there alone, him not looking at me and yet telling me about his day using baseball analogies. He hit a home run in a class. So and so on our dorm floor was like a shortstop, a cut off between the other players. He would advance someone in his estimation or let them strike out. They weren't exactly the sexy conversations of most college students. Home runs. Reaching second base, etc. His understandings were not sexual at all. He only used them as a familiar and safe way to explain himself.

Phil had been bullied in high school in an uncharacterstic way. He was completely ignored as if he didn't exist. He had no friends. Absolutely none. And he resented it. He was good looking and intelligent, but he could see neither because no one validated his existence or his gifts.

Phil had saved up all of his money to buy a Ford Mustang Cobra in high school, adding bells and whistles that no one considered. It was fast and immaculate. He hoped it would open conversations with students he wanted to befriend. They used him for rides, but friendships never materialized. I felt sorry for him so I decided to help him out. I knew I couldn't do it overtly. I had to ease my way with him. He didn't trust anyone.

The first time he actually looked at me was the night he was commenting on a game and the play just called. I opened up my knowledge about his favorite sport. "No," I corrected his interpretation of the coach's call, "that play was clearly not the right one. He should've thrown it into the second baseman while the short covered third."

"Well, how do you know that?"

"Because Phil, I have played the sport since I was in third grade."

What manifested in that conversation was a challenge. I dared him to sign up for the dorm's softball team and show me his skills. "Our floor is playing the other floors in Moore Hall. Sign up. We'll see who the better athlete is."

I knew what I was doing. He had no clue. Once he signed up, I was introducing him to his fellow floor mates.

After a grueling game, he rushed me on the field, "You are an incredible player!"

"Back atcha."

From that moment on, Phil attended parties with me. We kayaked together on the KAW River for our dorm invitational against other dorms. Since I had moved on campus that year and it was Phil's first year at college, every activity that spelled adventure, I encouraged him to try with me. I drove him to Matt's campus so they could meet. He drove me to his parents' summer home at the Lake of the Ozarks so we could take their boat out and ski.

**

Phil went from a shy, soft spoken hermit his freshman year to a dorm monitor his sophomore year. He was even a waiter for a popular restaurant at the lake that summer, where he met his future wife. And by my senior year, his junior, he had become an outspoken daredevil. He bought a motorcycle and we'd drive around town searching for places to pool hop after hours. Watching him dive, half-naked, off diving boards into the deserted pools, made me beam like a proud parent. He had arrived. When he joined the K-State trick water skiing club, I knew he was finally free of his social inhibitions. He was showing other people what he was made of. At skydiving, though, he balked.

"Come on, Phil. Imagine how much fun it will be. How others will look at us and think, *wow they have balls!*"

I explained that I was doing it to overcome my fear of heights. I failed to mention that I was afraid to go it alone.

I'm not sure which guilt-laden combination of coercion actually worked, but he made the decision. I think it was to master fears of his own.

Matt was even inspired to take the plunge. Except, he did it as a part of his Airborne training in the Army. Typical Matt, he had to do it before I did. He signed up the summer I was working to save the cash.

"Lisa, it was scary as hell. Not at first, but I had to make five jumps to qualify. On the fourth jump, my risers twisted and I flipped upside down. I was flying headfirst with pretty much a closed chute and the ground getting closer and closer."

"Oh god, what did you do?"

"I kicked my feet trying to right myself, thinking my kicking would untwist the risers, the chute would open and catch wind. I was freaking out. I finally got myself upright and the chute opened minutes before I hit the ground...hard." He was playing it out in his mind, I could tell, and nearly hyperventilating from the traumatic memory. "The shit part was that I had to get back up there the next day and do one last jump. I swear I didn't want it that bad, at that point."

"Man, I'm glad you're ok. How did you get yourself back up there?"

"I showed up and saw this other soldier, a girl, sobbing uncontrollably. She was so scared, but she showed up to jump. I found myself comforting her and encouraging her. When she jumped, I knew I could do it. Her courage inspired my own."

"Well…" I took a deep, weighted breath, "I'm still going to do it."

"Just be careful," he warned.

**

I attended the early skydiving instruction class, and Phil, the later. His architectural engineering classes ran all day. My science classes were all afternoon so I had my mornings free. There were only three classes before we risked our lives and limbs.

Our instructor, a disheveled and slight man, had been skydiving for twenty years. He greeted our class enthusiastically, "Skydiving is one of the safest sports." He was passionate and fired up. "I know what you've heard, but it's false. It's safer than scuba diving. It's the best experience you will ever have and if you listen to the instructions and exercise caution, you will minimize your risks. I'm not saying you will never have a bad dive. It happens. You do something long enough, your risks increase. But even having broken ribs myself after flying through a grove of trees, I still contend it's the best sport ever. It's a blast! Man, there is nothing like it!"

The rest of our days were spent in lectures that began with the sentence, "And if you don't do this, you will die…"

The one example I remember was the lady who didn't do one of her checks, turning her head side to side so that the parachute would catch wind and open. Paralyzed with fear, she never did the one thing that would've saved her life.

Our final class, we met at the airplane hangar our Cessna would be docked in. It was simulation day. Swings affixed to the hangar's ceiling by heavy chains ripped through my crotch like a wire diaper. There was nothing comfortable about it. Once secured, we practiced leaping off of a stack of cement blocks.

Our instructor took the time to explain the procedure to us. "When that plane door opens and you step out onto the wing, that's it. You have to jump. It's a safety hazard for us to let you back in. You could pull an unprepared diver out with you in your attempts to reenter the plane and we can't have that. So if you step onto the wing, you are committed at that point and there's no turning back. Once on the wing, you will be given the command "dot" and when you hear that, you let go of the plane's struts that you will be holding onto. If you hang on, you might run the risk of hitting high wires or trees, so go when you hear the signal."

Keeping all of that information straight when your life depends on it, is a terrifying responsibility.

The night before I was due to jump, I lay in my bed while my roommates slept and hugged my Bible, a cross and a lucky few items I intended to put in my socks. I nearly drown in my pool of nervous sweat. The phone rang at 6 a.m.

"Hey, we're not going to jump today. It's too windy. Not safe," my skydiving instructor informed me.

Phil called next, "I'm bummed that we're not jumping today. I was ready." I confessed that I was nervous and Phil reassured me that all was well. We'd be together and that's what friends are for.

I was concerned that I might forget the instructions in the week leading up to our next attempt. Even though it was a static line jump and a certain degree of control was in another's more experienced hands, I was scared.

The following week, on our reassigned jump day, I got a call bright and early.

"So, you still gonna skydive?" Mark. He still didn't believe me. He started singing, "I went to a funeral…."

"Look, knock it off. I'm jumping today."

"When?" I could hear the panic in his voice.

"In a couple of hours."

"Don't jump til I get there," he nearly screamed into the phone.

"I can't stop the plane from taking off."

"Hold them up. I'm coming."

It was a two hour drive and I was unsure if he'd make it.

"I'll be there. Just wait for me."

We hung up and I felt a little relieved. Thank God, family would be there. I always joke that he did it because he wanted to ensure that my music collection went to him in my will. I think he was actually concerned for me and my well being and had to be there as my big brother protector.

I drove to the airplane hangar, praying the whole way. Ben and my friend Tina met me there. Both wanted to support me in the jump. Phil showed up, sheet white and shaken. His fears had a chance to build up resistance over the week and his will was not as strong.

"We'll be fine, Phil. Together."

Mark showed up with my niece Ashley just as we were getting our jumpsuits on. Ashley was just 9 years old and followed me around asking questions. A more seasoned female jumper answered them for me.

"What's it like?" Ashley stared up to the woman with wonder.

The woman gave her a sanitized answer, then turned to me. "It's better than sex!"

Everyone laughed but Phil. He was fastening his jumpsuit and focusing. We put our helmets on, which were rigged with a walkie talkie inside for communication with an instructor on the ground, and wandered toward the plane. My friend Tina was snapping pictures and Ben waved. He was reassuring, but I could see his worry. My brother just shook his head in disbelief. Ashley was riveted with awe.

"Okay, gather around here," the dive instructor motioned to us. "All right, so we will be jumping by height..."

I looked around to Phil. Taller than me. And the other guy jumping with us. Taller than me. "Wait. So I'm going first?" I was stunned. I had planned on jumping last, able to take time to steel my nerves.

"You're up!" he laughed.

Oh shit. The panic set in again.

We received brief reminders about our safety checks and then I turned and waved to my supporters and hopped into the plane.

When the plane reached 3,260 feet, the instructor opened the Cessna's door. He made sure I was ready and I stepped out onto the wing. The wind, at that height, was cold and blustering. It blew the pant legs of my jumpsuit like a sailboat sail in a hurricane. The flapping was my initial distraction, but

I managed to hold on to the struts of the wing. I found myself staring down at the checkered pattern of the farmland below. I had only been in an airplane once, but I was too little to remember much. This time I knew exactly what was happening. I couldn't decide if that was a good thing or not.

"It looks like a quilt from up here!" I screamed over the sputter of the engine and the high velocity wind.

"Dot!"

"This is amazing! Beautiful!"

"Dot!"

I thought I heard the instructor's voice as the plane plugged along, heading toward the hangar, the trees and the power lines. I was enraptured by the view from that vantage point and forgot the command momentarily.

"DOT! DOT! DOT!"

I finally heard him and with a quick prayer, let go. I broke away from the airplane, falling behind it. I had a brief rush before the plane yanked my rip cord. I looked side to side and the chute, hovering in a ball behind my head, caught air and opened in full.

I could hear the command in my helmet, "Check your risers and be sure they're straight."

"Check," I called back.

From that point forward I fell like a feather, drifting side to side, straight into a ditch. I was screaming "Woo Hoo!" and "This is awesome!" the whole way down.

"You are having entirely too much fun with this," the voice in my helmet had laughed as he instructed me on how to toggle and have a little fun with the controls before my dive ended. When I landed, I pulled the chute off of me and fell back on the rough edged surface of a deep groove in the ground.

I saw my loved ones running towards me. They were cheering and offering me a hand when we heard Phil above us. He started his squealing, high pitched screams from the time the plane's door opened until he hit the ditch in nearly the exact same spot I did. I've never heard a swear word last that long. "Ohhhhhhhh…shiiiiiiiiiiiiit!"

When our final picture was taken with my family and friends, Phil and I were all smiles. We walked off, cocky, like we had the largest set of brass balls ever. Of course, I had to adjust my lucky charms, Bible and cross to make room for them.

My lasting memory, the photos taken by my friends and my dad's ultimate commemoration of the occasion- a personalized artist drawing of me falling from a plane into a ditch- gave me a reality check for an experience that was so surreal in the moment.

"I was so worried about you," my mom said quietly after it was all over.

"No need to worry, Mom. It was worth it." I murmured under

my breath, "Better than sex!"

YOU WON'T LEAVE HERE LIKE YOU CAME

By the time I reached my senior year at Kansas State University, I was more than ready to graduate and move on. The years between my fledgling attempts to master my grades as a freshman and the skills I'd acquired by my senior year, where I finally got my first 4.0 in a college semester, were dismal. I enjoyed the people I met and I did learn a few things, mostly about life.

I learned that I could have a safe cocktail and not miss a week of class because of it. How I ever pulled off my mandatory physical fitness class, hung over at 7 a.m. my freshman year, is a mystery. As is the passing grade I got for my 3 hour night time psychology class. I lapsed a few classes leading up to the final and walked in the night I would have to take it. I can only say that I yanked the essays from the nether regions of my anal sphincter and passed. I'm sure Freud would have something smart to say about that.

I eventually learned to cook efficiently. I made casseroles which lasted for a week, saving me valuable study time. I only varied my routine when Matt would come visit.

"Let's make a butt cookie!" I enticed him one day.

"You mean a big lump of dough?" Matt matched my enthusiasm.

"Yeah. You know how your mom would never let you just mix a big ball and make one giant cookie? Let's do that!"

The sad reality of that cooking extravaganza was that on a college budget, name brand chocolate chip cookie dough was unheard of. Matt and I pooled our change together and bought some pre-made powdered crap with slivers of "chocolate" chips mixed in.

"Whose butt should we mold it after, yours or mine?" Only Matt would consider this detail.

"Who do you want to mold it after?"

"Mine. I have a tattoo on my ass so that adds more ingredients," Matt suggested, brimming with hope.

"Ok, but yours is a heart so what are we going to use that's red?"

Without even a moment's consideration, he bursts, "Jelly!"

We molded a butt out of dough. With surgical detail, we made a freehand outline of a heart and filled it in with grape jelly. I placed our creation in the oven. Mmmm. Mmmm. Crap. The cookie had the consistency of sand paper and tasted the same.

Matt and I didn't attend the same university, but we managed to spend a lot of time together. Weekends of partying ending with a Sunday hibernation day, just the two of us, watching movies or making ass cookies. We were the last of our high school group of friends who still made the effort to hang out. It was a comfort during those college years to periodically see a familiar face.

Together, Matt and I managed a decent rapport with one another's new friends. My friend Ben and I drove down to see Matt at his college one lazy afternoon and found a refrigerator full of science experiments. Matt was majoring in zoology. A tray of insects pinned to a cardboard sheet took up a whole shelf in his refrigerator. Matt wasn't back from class yet, but true to his carefree spirit, the door was unlocked and he left a note saying, "Make yourselves at home."

Not like any home we'd ever been in. Ben re-opened the fridge and yanked out a curdled jug of some frothy beverage when Matt arrived home. "What's this?"

"Orange juice."

"Holy shit Matt, it's green! That. Is. Disgusting." Ben laughed.

"Yeah, well my maid is on vacation."

We looked to the carpet of clothes on the floor and laughed. Matt picked up a stray shirt near his recliner and sniffed it. He changed clothes and presented himself ready to go out to dinner with us.

"Sniff and Go," I laughed.

Mmmm. College.

The experience of college was bittersweet. A friend of mine was murdered my freshman year which escalated my grief and cast a haunting shadow over all of my experiences for years to come. I drank with the requisite gusto of my peers, but I truthfully never really enjoyed it. I drank to numb my reality in those years. My senior year I had made friends with a solid group of people, ambitious future health professionals like myself and an art student or two. We huddled together in quiet pubs and drank a few beers for the social aspect, rather than the drunken need to annihilate our senses. I had matured on that level.

Though Oceanography didn't reveal any good spring break spots, I'd taken a few of those to Panama City Beach, Florida. I saw the ocean for the first time and found a peace with her which has sustained me throughout my life, though I much prefer the Pacific to the Atlantic. Matt and I marveled the Pacific when we had occasion to vacation together. We were both giddy like children when we noticed that the sandy beaches of Gold Coast, Oregon illuminated with an electric blue hue wherever we walked. We had no idea what was causing it, but we stared at it for hours, strolling the coastline. On a subsequent spring break from my graduate studies, Matt had planned for us to ferry into Canada from Seattle where he had just taken a management position for a shipping company.

"Let's go to Tofino! It looks stunningly beautiful and I think you'll love it." He pulled up a website. "We can go whale watching and sea kayaking!"

"Sounds like a blast! Let's do it!"

We rented a convertible Mustang and with "Baby Got Back" blasting from the stereo, we were off on our adventure.

Tofino was a blissful trip compared to the spring breaks I'd taken while in undergrad. We stayed at a bed-and-breakfast and took in the one road town full of hippies and hikers.

Whale watching was educational, but the sea kayaking gave us a better view of the mammal, if only a terrorizing one. While manning our kayak together after a hike on the nearby Indian reservation, we hit a rough patch of water and couldn't get past the tide. While I struggled to paddle us in a suitable direction to get around it, Matt pedaled for speed. We had been warned that the gray whales were in season. We were instructed on how to flip our boats over should a whale emerge and capsize us. All very good in theory. When I saw the pinkish flesh of an enormous creature beneath the kayak and stopped paddling, all I heard was Matt screaming behind me, "Why did you stop? Keep paddling!"

"Whhh...whhh...whhh..." I couldn't squeak it out. "WHALE!" I finally managed to scream.

Matt froze with me and the kayak drifted backwards. The whale passed beneath us peacefully and kept moving. The only thing moving between Matt and I were our bowels.

**

I learned a lot from my excursions during college, but in my undergraduate classes, nothing really grabbed my attention. Oh sure, shattering roses and tennis balls in my chemistry classes using liquid nitrogen was exhilerating. My general physics class with a hyperactive, hippy naturalist was enjoyable. I could even say that I liked anatomy. But my senior year was when my reasons for attending college finally fell together in some premonitory way.

I had a class with Dr. Karla Kubitz, a health conscious alternative medicine advocate from Arizona State University. She studied under Dr. Andrew Weil, MD, a nationally recognized holistic physician. I didn't know who he was at the time.

Dr. Kubitz taught sports psychology, but in the most unique way. She was a meditative energy in a classroom of gym rats. She taught us visualization techniques and progressive relaxation. I knew nothing of either. Dr. Kubitz never told us what she was doing when she'd have us close our eyes and then lead us through a guided meditation. I found my whole body tingling when she finished each session. Those experiences were foundational in more than just a physical or academic way, it was grounds for the spiritual inner knowingness I'd be enhancing in the years to come.

Dr. Kubitz took to me immediately. When she found out I was doing stand-up comedy, she asked me to teach one of her classes on topic.

"I would love for you to share with the class how humor is therapeutic and how it can be used to heal. Most of this class will go on and become health professionals. Laughter will be invaluable. I think you will do wonderfully. I'll give you extra credit to do it."

I prepared a speech that mentioned Norman Cousins, who had cured himself of a debilitating illness through laughter. The exact diagnosis is still under debate, but by his decision to include comedic movies and trained laughter into a healthy regimen of proper nutrition and attitude, he literally laughed himself to health. I asked the class to participate in exercises designed to churn the creative juices of their own senses of humor.

As a result of my dedication and overachieving in Dr. Kubitz's class, I aced it. As for the guided meditations and visualization exercises, I could only thank her years later when I understood the gift she'd offered me.

Dr. Saturn didn't hold the same appeal for me. She was a strict, moody woman who never bent when it came to her class requirements. She was extremely hard on me during her Biomechanics class, but she was very pleasant when I would find myself conferencing with her about my grades in her office, which was often. She knew I could do better. So did I.

When I finally walked in to drop her class, she seemed genuinely hurt and wanted me to stick it out.

"I don't want a C. I need my grades to reflect my ability and especially since I will be going on to physical therapy school."

She discouraged me from dropping her class, but I refused to budge. Unlike the retake courses, dropping a class was a clean slate, however, a waste of money. I paid for all of my education so it would only be hurting me. I didn't feel the guilt that others did when they failed or dropped a class and their parents had to pony up the money for another round.

"I really wish you'd reconsider," she said it with a hint of concern, but I could tell she approved of my decision. She held back what appeared to be a look of pride on her face that I was such a dedicated student.

"No, I'm a better student than this grade reflects."

She gave me a tight smile, but a smile nonetheless. "I respect your decision."

What I didn't know was that I'd have the joy of having her for two classes the next semester. No one told me she taught a sports management class. Damn. Not only did I have to trace the anatomical movements of athletes, using a computer that looked like a viewmaster, for Biomechanics. But I had to design a sporting facility for her management class as well.

In Biomechanics, I would study sporting maneuvers on the computerized slides, place trace paper over the screen and then draw out every change in arc of their movements. I then prepared papers which stated whether the athlete used the proper angle for the move. I'd spend hours in the lab measuring and assessing the likelihood of the successful completion of each action during an actual game scenario. I would also have to note the anatomical body part used, its range of comfortable motion and the muscles involved. There was plenty of math computations and anatomy, but the Laws of Physics also couldn't be ignored. It was a tough class, but I did exceptional work the second…well, first time I completed it.

Dr. Saturn taught her management class in the same dictatorial, complex fashion that she taught Biomechanics. In management class, we had to design a facility and research all of the components and cost of the materials to build it, then write up a proposal for how we'd ask a bank for the money. My team built a rock star fitness club, replete with floors that bounced and accommodated the movements involved in an aerobics class. The forgiving floors were gentler on the knees. As fate would have it, I was employed by a fitness club in high school and had always worked construction jobs with Mark to help him fund nursing school. I mostly painted, but I understood construction. Dr. Saturn loved that I included the proper biomechanical set up in my approach and gave me an A.

Ironically, I would be leading a step aerobics class on campus the very next semester when a loud pop would crumble me to the floor. My knee gave out under the pressure of the university's concrete subfloors. I had to undergo surgery just before graduation. I was still allowed to participate in my commencement exercises on time, but once again, I had to take late finals during the summer. Unlike my freshman year, however, I was allowed to take them all and passed them without incident.

The worst experience I ever had in all of my years at K-State was dealt by an art instructor on campus, a tenured professor who set up a separate final for the football players in our class. They were going to Japan to play and needed passing grades to participate. The class satisfied a mandatory humanities credit for pre-med/health science students. Half of the class was comprised of these future health professionals, like myself, who needed the grades to get into our respective schools. The rest of the class was mostly the football guys. I had no issues with the athletes. I'd tutored some of them and liked them, but favoritism when my grades are at stake? Not a fan.

The instructor graded on a bell curve. She gave the future doctors, nurses and therapists an impossible exam and recorded C's and lower in the grade books. It was my understanding that she passed the football boys with A's and B's.

A student who sat next to me for many of my classes showed me the test her boyfriend took on a random Saturday with the rest of his football buddies. It was an extremely easy test.

"He said that she walked them through it and gave them the answers on top of it all. I'm going to talk with her today and let her know that I know and I'd better not get a bad grade. I need to keep my scholarship."

I was stunned. Politics? On campus? Surely not.

This girl planned to help the rest of us out. Our very next class with the teacher, the girl looked smugly satisfied. I approached her and took a seat next to her moments before our last class began. Just as the instructor started answering questions about the results of our final, I turned to the girl, "So, how did it go?"

"Oh, she gave me my B," the girl spoke with attitude.

"And what about the rest of us?"

She looked apologetic, but it was contrived. "I can't. I'm sorry. I promised her I wouldn't let anyone else in on it." She frowned at me, not a trace of guilt. "It's the only way I can keep my scholarship."

So much for learning to do the right thing. I was pissed.

The rest of the health care degree seeking students gathered together and formed an alliance. We would take turns confronting this issue and push it as far as we must to get justice. Within the first week, I was alone in the pursuit. Everyone gave up.

"This is bullshit!" I cried.

And they nodded and sucked up their defeat.

"Screw her. She can't do this."

And they agreed and walked back to the administration building to enroll in the class again.

I made waves. Tidal waves, if I remember my Oceanography class notes correctly. Only my wave wasn't pulled by the moon, but rather my moods, swinging indiscriminately imbalanced by the scales of injustice. I went above the instructor's head. I raged to one higher up after another. They insisted I speak with her. It's protocol.

"Why would I speak with her? She's unreasonable, obvious from her corrupt actions."

The academic deans maintained I'd get further if I chose to leap through the hoops. So I did.

She was furious the afternoon I confronted her and accused her of cheating her best students out of their grades. Then I land blasted her with the secondary test I was aware the football boys had taken.

"How do you know about that?" she hissed.

"It doesn't matter. It's true, isn't it?"

She was shaking with rage. "How dare you…" she started to attack.

"How dare YOU is the better question. I hope you get fired for this." I knew she wouldn't. Tenure. Whatever.

I stormed out and walked straight into my academic advisor's office. Dr. Nancy Bouchier was a hippy Canadian. She drove a Harley Davidson to school every day, smoking cigars, her long hair whipping in the wind like an afterthought.

Dr. Bouchier taught a sports history class that forced me to dig through Galileo's theories and render an opinion.

"It's mostly crap," I said in my barely fertile experience on the chosen topics.

I was outspoken, which she appreciated, but she smiled with a look that implied I'd learn more and when I did, I would see the error in my thinking. It would take years.

Dr. Bouchier stared at me that day in her office. I was nearly unhinged with anger.

"Lisa…" she began gently, "I can't tell you what to do. I know you're upset. I would be, too. The fact is, though, your degree is under the umbrella of the Athletic Department. If you make too many waves, they will make it hell for you to graduate. You are approaching your senior year, do you really want that?"

I was still too pissed to focus.

She continued, "If you need to do it and speak your peace, of course you can go to the University Court and plead your case, but I'd think it through."

She counseled me on several more occasions, but I'd already called one of my favorite advisors, Ms. B.

"Lisa…" That familiar voice instantly made me feel safe. "You will learn in life that you just have to take things as far as you're comfortable. And when you're satisfied that you've done everything that you can do, then you have to let it go."

I knew she was right.

I pushed it a little further and when I got no result, I didn't press it. I let it go.

I graduated from Kansas State University and moved on with my life. I never joined their alumni association and I vowed to never give them a dime of my money. It was a promise I made myself. With years, I've softened. Most recently, I have considered a donation, but something always stops me. I know one day, I will open my heart and that door once again, but it's a process. An apology from the university and a change of my grade would have certainly helped. I'm sure that the art teacher didn't come up with that whole idea on her own. And though it would've been so easy to point a finger at the football program itself, I knew it didn't come from there. Having worked a season within Coach Snyder's staff, the head football coach at the time, I knew he had too much integrity to sanction such behavior. You couldn't have convinced me that the art teacher had any such integrity. In my eyes, the entire blame rested on her shoulders back then. I wanted to hate her for tampering with my GPA that I'd worked so hard to build up.

Packing up my belongings to move home for a brief time while I considered my future, I remembered a humble little retreat I attended my sophomore year with some dorm buddies. It was for a church youth group and though I couldn't tell you a thing about the actual camp (too preachy), I can say it's where I saw a sign whose message struck my memory for years.

"You won't leave here like you came, In Jesus Name. Tortured, sick, blind or lame. You won't leave here like you came, In Jesus Name."

And I didn't, for better or worse, leave K-State like I came.

DEAR GOD

My trusted companion, Mom, drove with me to a small Missouri town called Boliver. I had been accepted into the physical therapy program at a small Christian college, Southwest Baptist University, and I wanted to tour the campus. The drive was a heavenly blend of nature's best foliage with a touch of hillbilly Ozark magic. Billboards for artisan gifts, Mom and Pop stores and down home cookin' lined the highways. It's what my Nanny would've called a place where the "hoot owls do the chickens dirty."

Mom and I haggled over directions, but once we arrived in the tiny town, our moods changed. It was a quaint little place and she was more excited than I'd imagined at the prospect of me being further educated in this wholesome environment.

We toured the campus and walked through the dorms I'd be sharing with three other female students.

"Visiting hours for male companions are over at 8 p.m," our guide informed us.

That was a twist. Coming from K-State where guys roamed the

hallways of both male and female corridors freely- sometimes clothed, sometimes not- this would be an adjustment.

"You will be enrolled in mandatory religion classes every semester," my guide told me. I wasn't opposed, but it did seem a bit invasive. I wasn't Baptist, but I was told that it didn't matter. The university welcomes everyone. *Except males in the female receiving dorms at hours past 8*, I made the mental contradiction.

A few weeks after I had returned home, nursing my mixed emotions about my decision, I received a sobering letter.

The university had been denied accreditation for their physical therapy program. The American Physical Therapy Association took exception to the religion requirements, stating that they could not allow the curriculum for their degree track to be altered. It would not be fair comparatively to the students undergoing training in other universities that offered the degree.

Even with the final line stating that my acceptance was guaranteed and I would be notified when they had worked out the issue, I was heartbroken.

I yanked a lined sheet of paper out of a leftover notebook from K-State and began writing a thoughtful letter to God. I explained my hurt feelings. Asked for guidance. I closed with a request that I be led to the places and people that would expand my spiritual path and help me grow.

Ben, my friend from K-State, called within a week. "Hey, Lis.

I heard about the PT thing. Sorry about that. Hey, I was thinking, since you're going to need a few more requirements than you got at good old KSU, how about you move to Kansas City and join me? I found a program that is an 8-week intensive for health professionals. It's a pre-pro program. It's designed specifically to fill in the gaps of the most common classes required to get you on your path. You could finish up Physics 1 and 2 and Organic Chemistry 1 and 2. I think they even offer Cell Biology. What do you say? Wanna be roommates?"

"Let me take some time to think it over."

"Well, don't take too long. Classes start soon."

I had enrolled in a computerized statistics course at a local community college in my hometown. We had just wrapped up and I thought attending this Donnelly College with Ben might be a decent option.

"Just while you're waiting to hear back from your PT school," Ben had pointed out.

I was bored at home and used to my freedom, so I eventually agreed. Ben was right. I needed the classes anyway, so why not?

Living with Ben was nothing like I expected. The perk was that I had someone to share expenses with and who valued studying like I did. The down side was his obsessive need to clean every inch of the apartment. Every day. I didn't bring many things with me when I moved in: a bed, dresser, books and some clothes. He brought the dishes and furniture along with his personal effects. He polished and cleaned them neurotically.

It's not like I was a slob, but Ben was an anal retentive neat freak. Before I could even rest a dirty dish in the sink to be placed in the dishwasher later, Ben had lifted it, scoured it and put it back in its place.

My final roommates at K-State were two girls I'd met in the dorms and a guy that I lovingly say, "Came with the apartment." Pete had lived with the former tenants, whom I knew, and the landlord told me he had dibs. If I was okay living with him, she was willing to work with me on rent.

Pete was a nightmare of a roommate in the cleanliness department. He would leave dishes lying around in his room until fur grew over the molded remnant of dinners' past. His disordered room looked like Matt's former apartments, but even Matt got his tidy act together after some military training. He was a dutiful housekeeper by the time I visited him in his first apartment post-college. Pete never got his act together while we were roommates. He was a cool guy, a former Coast Guard, who had tragically lost his best friend in a Florida hurricane. Grief and depression is what I would attribute to his disregard for tidiness now. Then, my roommates and I would've considered him slovenly. If we mopped the floor, within hours, he'd track his muddy bike tires through the kitchen. Just a nightmare.

It was Mark who pointed out the less obvious consideration. "You're living with a guy? Well, just remember all guys pee in the shower. ALL guys."

I stocked up on Dow bathroom cleaner from that point forward. Since Pete and I shared the downstairs shower, I sprayed it down every morning before I ever stepped foot inside of it. One of my female roommates laughed at the whole idea and considered herself lucky that she didn't have to share with Pete. She didn't laugh nearly as hard as I did because I remembered that our other roommate had confessed that she peed in the showers in the dorm. It's still funny to me when I think about it.

If Pete was on a sliding scale tilted toward filth, Ben was compulsively over board on the opposing end. Not a speck of our apartment was out of place. It was like being a guest in my own home every day. If it's true that cleaniless is next to godliness, Ben was approaching sainthood.

I was grateful when my friend Jamie from high school came to visit with his new girlfriend and noticed the same thing I did. "Wow...this apartment is..." he fumbled for a word, "sterile." He laughed a bit. "I feel like I'm in a hospital."

"I know, right?"

The good news was that Ben was hardly ever around. His girlfriend was attending college in a nearby school and he stayed most nights at her house. I was elated with the additional perk.

When school started, Ben and I drove up to meet with the head of the program, Dr. Delta Gier. He was a Darwinian looking man who smoked a pipe and called everyone "cherub." He was a noted chemist who had called the likes of Dr. Albert Einstein friend and was chummy with another fellow I'd heard of before. "Dr. Andrew Weil and I are friends. I go fishing with him every summer," he told me.

I knew I was led to the right place.

Our visit to the financial aid advisor was even more enlightening for me. Walt was gay. I knew it right off. Ben didn't. I sat with my new roommate throughout his financial interview, at his request, and heard Walt spray our conversation with shallow flattery directed at Ben.

"So how many loans have you taken out so far?" he asked Ben.

Ben answered while Walt gazed lovelorn at his lanky features. When he'd finished the business at hand, Walt spun his onyx pinky ring and clasped his hands together. Oh good, I thought, social hour was about to begin.

"So, Ben, you sure are a tall drink of water. How tall are you?"

"6 foot."

"Mmmm. Hmmmm." Walt kept his eyes fixated on Ben in the most delightfully inappropriate way. "And how long are your legs?"

I nearly crashed under my chair laughing.

"Time to go, Lis. I'll meet you outside."

"Ewww, I love it when they squirm," Walt laughed and gave me a wink.

Ben grabbed me by the shoulders when I walked out of Walt's office, still laughing. "That guy is…"

"Wonderful," I said giggling.

Ben didn't share my joy, but over time, he grew to adore Walt as the rest of us did. Walt was harmless and extremely funny. Best yet, if he liked you, he rushed your student loans through and had them in your hot hands in a flash.

I met some wonderful spiritual people at that school who helped me evolve my own spirit in ways I'm yet processing. Most of the students were older and either starting late careers in health care or returning to school to advance their studies. I learned a lot from them. Most of them had heard of Dr. Gier. Some traveled a great distance to be in his presence. I was one of the rare few who had no idea who he was or how blessed I was for having him.

He rarely taught a class, but when he filled in for O-Chem, it was a baffling study for me. In letters and numbers that looked like peck marks, he filled the chalkboard with formulas that canvassed the entire space. I had no idea what it all meant. Only one person understood enough to even ask a question.

When Dr. Boudrum, our regular Organic Chemistry instructor returned, we bombarded him with our confusion. We had serious questions that tended to last the whole class period. Boudrum was an adorable little Indian man. He had a sweet accent and though I hardly understood a word of his lectures, I did learn a lot in the class. Mostly from other students and a rigorous studying effort on my part.

It's why I was so shocked to walk into class one day and have him wield a brick at me. I ducked and flattened myself on the floor before I heard the hysterical laughter of my classmates. The brick was a realistic foam replica.

"They tell me to do it. They tell me..." he pointed to my friends in the front row "....they say, 'throw it at Lisa.' They tell me."

"Mmmm. Hmmm. Likely," I muttered, amused. "I think you wanted to throw it at me the whole time."

He laughed, but not nearly as loud as the suave Mexican guy named Miguel, who had a Desi Arnez chortle which inspired others to laugh with him. He always put his hands on my shoulders and talked like a used car salesman. He was headed to medical school, but I'd later catch up with him in chiropractic college.

Dr. Gier had that way of redirecting your course. He told one of my friends that she was headed to naturopathic college when she'd already told him she was looking into medical programs.

"I'm going to be an MD," she politely corrected him.

"That's what I said, cherub, ND."

I told him I was going to be a PT.

"A DC! Wonderful!"

"What's a DC?"

"A Doctor of Chiropractic. You'll be wonderful at it," he encouraged.

He told Miguel he saw him as a DC as well and soon enough, it manifested.

For me, the journey was longer and took more convincing. My new friend Robert, a Hawaiian who loved natural medicine, lauded praises over chiropractic and the holistic leanings of an MD named Deepak Chopra. Doors opened in my awareness that I never considered. One of my best friends in the program, Raina, also a future chiropractor, bestowed the virtues of the field upon me. My best friend Taylor was too busy teaching the rest of the students what we were supposed to be learning in our classes to offer a redirect on my career choice.

Taylor was especially adept at tutoring physics, which was taught by another entertaining instructor named Mr. Maples. He didn't take us anywhere near seriously. He taught physics straight out of the textbook and often, in his high pitched voice would turn to our class and begin a lecture, "You might recall from your organic chemistry class…" then with a quick perusal of our baffled faces, he'd continue, "or perhaps not." He'd start the lecture, assuming we'd learned nothing.

I feverishly made note cards and tried to learn anything I could from the program, but I just didn't find the education there. This was a course load designed to move you along to your next destination. It had nothing to do with actually mastering the material. I was disappointed with that aspect, but I did enjoy my fellow students. I made lots of life long friends.

Raina was a particularly fun friend acquisition. She and I studied together a lot. She was a task master and stayed focused, but she struggled. I had a handle on most of the material, but I struggled, too, even though I pulled out A's and B's. On one particular test, we enlisted a fellow student to help us study. Kristin was in her late 30's and had no idea what she wanted to be when she grew up. She did, however, have a handle on how to explain most anything in a way Raina understood.

Just before our physics final, Kristin explained to Raina how to remember a certain concept about inertia. "It's like the Flintstones," she started. "Say you have Fred Flintstone, rolling down the hill in his rock wheeled car, and there's Dino hanging out the back." Kristin had children and her analogy reflected that. Raina grasped the cartoon concept right off, but struggled to apply it. I figured out how to apply the physics terms we were introduced to in class and tried to help her.

When the final was over, Taylor, Kristin and I waited in the hallway. Everyone was curious to know how Raina did. When she finished, we met her at the door.

"So? How did you do?" Kristin nearly lunged at her.

As luck would have it, the concept Kristin had explained was on the test.

"I remembered what you said," Raina explained. "I kept coming back to that question throughout the whole exam."

"So what did you write?" Kristin hurried her along.

"I started with…so, say you have Fred Flintstone…"

We were laughing. Surprisingly, she got partial credit. Only because Mr. Maples was too amused to give her a zero for that question. Instead, he wrote her a special note, "Very entertaining."

Mr. Maples showed his support for me by showing up to one of my stand-up comedy shows. I was pleasantly surprised to see him sitting in the front row with the rest of my friends, indulging himself in a cocktail. It was the first time I realized that teachers are people, too.

What I had gained from my experiences in that program brought warm memories of high school back to me. The smaller school helped to foster an environment of friendships and camaraderie. Those connections lasted longer than the memory of what I learned there. In fact, it was the lesson. In time, I realized that those beautiful souls were the answer to the prayerful letter I'd written to God.

EVEN THE DOG KNEW

As an intern at Cleveland Chiropractic College, I was plagued by perpetual nervous energy. I tried to juggle classes, schedule appointments with my patients, fulfill clinical requirements for graduation and fine tune the skills that would make me an effective, skilled doctor. The doctor I dreamed I could be.

When I was a child, I considered being a doctor and life bumped me along various roads until I made the decision. I abandoned my pursuit of physical therapy school when I met those outstanding future doctors of chiropractic at Donnelly. I reevaluated why I wanted to go into health care originally. I wanted to assist people on their healing journey and I wanted to help my loved ones who needed it, especially my brother Mark. He has a health condition that I thought could benefit greatly from chiropractic care. I considered that chiropractic encompassed my beliefs about life and wellness and, more specifically, spirituality. A natural approach that allows the body the chance to heal itself, when restfully unimpeded, seemed like just what the body is innately designed to do. I supported the idea of proper biomechanics, nutrition and energy which lifts it into that homeostatic state.

At some point, I just knew I would go to chiropractic college. I was finally ready to commit. What I wasn't ready for was life's curve balls I endured while in chiropractic school. Relationships headed on a fast track to disaster. An unexplained illness had me doubting myself as a doctor and losing valuable class time. The lack of support from my loved ones for my chosen career path (all except my mom who lovingly supported me from day one) was an especially hurtful surprise. It was difficult to embrace those loved ones who gave me their bipolar input on a regular basis. One day, "We're so proud of you." The next, "Why don't you become a *real* doctor?"

On top of the other stressors, I was carrying more hours than I ever had in any academic curriculum, and struggling to keep my head above water with all of the distractions.

The only thing that made it bearable was having a few gifted and caring instructors during my doctoral pursuit. I did have a few duds, but that was to be expected.

I spent time with a few chosen instructors outside of class. They didn't strike me as professors, but friends. Most instructors, I simply had no desire to engage in anything other than a professional relationship. It didn't mean I didn't respect them as peers. I did. I just couldn't see myself trespassing the lines of a social engagement.

One such instructor that will always stand out for his polarizing disposition was Dr. Hugo Gibson. He was South African and had an accent that was dazzling and engaging. His darling silver hair layered just so and his dress code was sophisticated. Every day he wore a suit and tie. He kept his fingernails meticulously manicured and wore a striking watch and rings to accentuate his fine taste. He was a man's man, discussing the days when DC's and MD's nearly brawled at pubs every night after classes over their differing philosophies.

Not surprisingly, Dr. Gibson taught Chiropractic Philosophy. I found the material dry. It didn't really spell out our profession's philosophy at all, in my opinion. Or maybe it just didn't spell out mine. I was not enamored with the class. I was enthralled, however, with how animated he was in teaching it. He might have embellished a few stories, but he fired everyone up about chiropractic and no one could deny him that.

My favorite story was one he launched into every semester. Every student who had him for class knew the tale. "There I was, face to face with this snarling beast. He was glaring at me, his frothy spittle drizzling to the floor. I walked right over to him, grabbed right onto him and gave him a cervical adjustment that shook him to the soul. Afterwards, he stared me straight in the eyes and then licked my hand and wagged his tail. Even…the dog…knew the power of chiropractic."

My friend I'll call Sam, elbowed me in the rib cage. Both of us suspected it was bullshit, but we laughed anyway.

I had Dr. Gibson for my first adjusting class. It would not prove to be the technique I used, but I rather enjoyed Hugo's approach. He was fluid in his protocol and knew the nuances of the technique inside out. He taught us the maneuvers with skilled hands and worked with us until we could administer the adjustment with confidence. His grace and subtle touches made for a brilliant presentation. We were instructed to mimic him perfectly or risk failing his final assessments.

I was in love with the old fella. Oh not in a sexual way. I'd already discovered a lot about myself in that department. Though I will say, his silver hair was rather dreamy. I was mostly enamored with his confidence, however intimidating it was for his students.

The day he won me over was the day he observed me in our technique lab class and gave me the go ahead to adjust my patient. I fired a thrust that shook my anconeus muscle and clunked my patient's vertebra into place. Enthusiasm rippled throughout the classroom.

"That's an ass kicker, there. Right there," he pointed to me.

Ass Kicker. Yeah. That's the reputation I desired. It's how I wanted to be known. Dr. Ass Kicker. It hid the squirm in my gut that I was anything, but that.

Dr. Gibson and I formed an unshakable bond. He understood me. I wouldn't know that until I reached clinical rounds. Feeling understood was worth its weight in gold to me because throughout my years at chiropractic college, I had noticed that no one really did fully understand or appreciate me.

I rushed into the clinic one afternoon, as I was prone to do, preparing for my allotted time treating patients. After doing the requisite sign-in procedures to clock my hours, I hurriedly pulled the chart for my first patient of the day. She would be arriving in a half hour. I pulled the mandatory gown for her and waited nervously. I listened acutely for my name to be announced over the overhead speakers as I secretly chewed my nails in the student doctors' lounge downstairs.

I could feel the butterflies in my stomach. No matter how many times I treated a patient early on in my clinical experience, I still felt the need to wipe the wetness from behind my ears. I hadn't quite mastered the skill level I felt I needed to feel confident as a physician, but then I have incredibly high expectations of what mastery involves. Some of my peers, whether they felt their insecurities or not, had grasped the concept long ago that patients listen to a confident health care provider. It sets the patient's mind at ease to see confidence, if only the illusion of it. It didn't mean that these future docs had mastered their potential skill level yet, it just meant they knew enough to push their ego out in front of their fears. Some were downright arrogant.

Every doctor has a phase where they doubt themselves. Doctors are human. People tend to forget that, including the doctors themselves. Even though most of us logically assume there has to be a transitional time between being a student and becoming the doctor we've studied to be, patients expect us to have all of the answers. There are a few doctors who take that assumption and run with it, purporting they do, indeed, have them all. Somewhere between patient expectations and the truth of a physician's expertise is the balancing point. You have to know enough to treat a patient and yet be honest enough to admit when you don't, if only to yourself. Then be responsible enough to research or refer to someone who does know.

As an intern, you fumble with all aspects of care until you get it right. You're learning exactly what to say to a patient and what protocol to use. And you're never sure, not 100%, because you're still learning. Experience helps with the transition, but as every instructor will tell you, "They don't call your business a 'practice' for nothing."

Thankfully, as an intern, you have trained field doctors with years of experience to help you and back you up. Even so, it did little to ease my mind. I feared making mistakes. I didn't want anyone to fall through the cracks. I desired to do my best and be my best and I couldn't do it if I felt I was on shaky ground in any way. It was an impossible standard of care to set for myself.

Little did I know then, that I knew everything I needed to know to reason out a course of treatment. I just didn't trust myself yet. I was afraid. I just wasn't sure of what.

I heard my name called that day in the clinic indicating that my patient was, at last, there. I sped to the front desk. The chiropractic assistants signed off on the necessary paperwork and handed them back.

I walked into the waiting room and greeted my patient. The woman, who had been unable to walk without pain the week prior, moved a bit swifter right before my very eyes and followed me to the room I'd chosen for her adjustment.

Once within the safety of the treatment room, I took some brief notes based on her subjective statements as to how she was feeling.

"I've been pain-free the entire week since our last visit," she told me excitedly.

She had returned to all of her daily activities and even now, though her pain returned slightly from overdoing it the day before, she felt it wasn't nearly as severe.

"On a scale of 1-10, 10 being the worst pain you've ever felt, how would you rate your pain today?" I had to follow the clinic protocol by officially asking. I sat on a stool in front of her, head bowed and ready to write her response.

She gave me an answer that showed marked improvement. I still couldn't accept it as proof that I was doing a decent job. Instead, I focused on how much more I could do to help her. It was just not good enough for me to assure myself that I was providing great care, no matter how vast the improvement had been or how gleeful she was about her results.

I handed my patient the breezy gown with the embarrassing opened flap in back, walked out into the hallway and closed the door to allow her privacy.

I sought a clinician on the floor to sign off on my paperwork before administering treatment. I dreaded going into the hallway because I knew Dr. Gibson was lurking around and he still intimidated me at this point. Sure enough, there he stood in front of me without a single strand of that silver, shiny hair out of place. He drummed his trim fingernails on the clinician's table waiting to be of assistance to any intern in need. He adjusted his starched white doctor's coat and straightened his perfectly straight tie once for good measure. No doubt a dry cleaned suit hid beneath his smock. Dr. Gibson was always a presence.

He turned to me and smiled. "Do you need something signed?" his voice carried throughout the entire clinic floor.

"Yes," I replied more confidently than I felt.

He gingerly grabbed the chart from my clammy hands and whipped his signature on the appropriate line. When he finished, he smacked the point of his designer pen behind his name, leaving a pronounced period at the end and handed the chart back to me.

"Do you know why I ended my signature with a period?" He peered into me.

"No," I shook my head, a faint smile on my face.

"Because it's a statement."

Before I could respond, another intern had cornered him to sign off on his paperwork. I walked away and adjusted my patient, not quite sure what to think of his comment.

The adjustment I gave that day was smooth and flawless. The woman's eyes lit up with excitement at being able to rise from the adjusting table unassisted.

"That was a wonderful adjustment. You are a true healer."

I instantly looked away. I couldn't accept her compliment.

She reached for my hand with her weathered elderly hands as I tried to busy myself with more paperwork. "I mean it. You ARE a healer. You have the gift."

I forced myself to make eye contact and smiled into her kind eyes. She wouldn't allow me to disregard her compliment. It's rude to do that anyway and I know it, but it's hard to accept when you're not feeling on top of your game.

I drove home that night pondering Dr. Gibson's actions and words that afternoon. I could've dismissed it as arrogance. I gave him the benefit of the doubt because his idea intrigued me. I even amused myself as I drove with the idea that if I signed my name and ended with a symbol, what would it be? Most days, I decided it was a question mark. Sometimes, I thought it was an exclamation point. Other times an ellipsis, just three little dots leading to infinity. I had never considered it would end in a period. I couldn't confirm that my name made any sort of statement. I could see that Dr. Gibson was making a point. His name meant something. His life meant something. He affirmed that he was making a statement with both.

It would be another week before I'd have occasion to run into Dr. Gibson again. I had been particularly self-abusive this day and had all but decided that I wasn't meant to be a doctor. I had made a few frustrating mistakes on some paperwork that I couldn't just chalk up to error and let go of. I went to the extreme. My mind ran the toxic chatter of, *can't you get anything right?* and *maybe you're not good enough to be a doctor.*

My thoughts were cruel and punishing. I was ashamed that I felt that way about myself and more ashamed that I'd made a mistake. My thoughts were wreaking havoc with my self-esteem.

I tried to hide from everyone on this particular day, especially Dr. Gibson. I knew he was on shift and it was inevitable that I'd have to face him. I just didn't feel strong enough to hear anyone else besides me dish out the scathing reprimand I felt I deserved.

Hide as I may, I instinctively knew he would find me. It didn't prevent me from ducking behind corners, hoping not to cross his path, praying to find another clinician to sign off on my paperwork. With every turn, there he stood. I caught my peers hiding with me. Grown adults clinging to one another's doctor's coats like Scooby Doo and Shaggy, hoping we didn't have to face our fears of the distinguished biped that lay in wait for us, stalking the hallways. Interns pretended to busy themselves in the therapy bays as a decoy to mask their true intentions of avoiding Gibson. We'd all take off and disperse in different directions when we'd hear him whistling his way through the halls, making rounds about the circular design of the main clinic floor.

In hindsight, our behavior was silly. Why on earth were we so afraid of him? He was a good doctor, very knowledgeable, compassionate and passionate about chiropractic. We were simultaneously awed and terrified of him. We refrained from joking around him. He took chiropractic too seriously for that, we decided. To joke would seem like an insult. His integrity demanded a hushed, respectful demeanor from us all. We were hushed all right, this particular day, as none of us wanted to be found in our elaborate game of hide and seek.

I popped my head out of a treatment room and eyed the north corridor of the clinic hallway. It was empty. I could hear him discussing a chart with a fellow peer. I swore that he was on the west wing. I knew the coast would be clear so I made a break for it. I rounded the east entrance and realized that I'd miscalculated his exact coordinates on the clinic floor. Damn the acoustics in that building. His voice had carried on the lilting breezes of rapidly moving interns trying to dodge him. It had fooled me into believing he was on the west side of the clinic floor when, in fact, he sat right there in one of the padded chairs reserved for clinicians at the entrance to the east wing. I turned to run back the way I came when I heard a booming voice behind me.

"Ms. Hopkins?" He never referred to any of us as a doctor. Not until we earned the privilege.

I stopped dead in my tracks, frozen in my concrete faux leather uppers. I turned to see his cherubic, alabaster face glowing, his penetrating blue eyes looking right through me.

"Yes," I spoke meekly.

"Where are you going in such a hurry?"

I cursed the fact that I'd been singled out of the pedestrian rush hour as my peers made a break for it. Those lucky bastards made it to the clearing I was heading for myself just moments before. Damn. I saw my hopes fading.

"I...well...I," I stammered. "I have to go correct this paperwork. I made a horrible mistake and I feel terrible about it." My face fell. Ruby red cheeks, flushed with humiliation, replaced the distracted, worried frown I'd worn all day.

He didn't flinch at my admittance. He actually continued smiling. I couldn't stop the bounding pulse throbbing in my carotid arteries. I stood before him, motionless, quite shocked that I'd surrendered my grievance so effortlessly.

"Do you have time for a story?" his authoritative voice summoned.

I knew that there was only one answer and it wasn't no. "Sure," I spoke dejectedly.

"When I was a young man living in South Africa," he folded his hands across his chest, "I had just started my first job. I was 20 years old then." He didn't blink as he held my gaze.

I was about to collapse from the rigidly held stance I was barely holding. He didn't seem to notice.

"I had been raised to do everything perfect. My father was a perfectionist. Every night he would stay late cleaning every inch of the office he worked in. He'd organize and reorganize everything. There was not a paper out of place. You could eat crumbs off the floor, it was that clean. He was damn good at his job and very well respected." Dr. Gibson unfolded his hands and leaned back in his chair, still not breaking his visual grip on me.

"I learned that sort of perfectionism from him. When I got my first real job, I carried that dedication for doing a perfect job with me. One day, I made a mistake. A big mistake. I had screwed up some paperwork that I knew would take hundreds of follow up papers just to correct the error. I rushed to my immediate supervisor and told her. She looked at me like I'd lost my mind and told me to just correct the damn thing. I pleaded with her that I'd made a horrible mistake. She repeated herself, 'Just correct the damn thing.' I was pissed off. I walked to the office of the main supervisor, my boss's boss. I told him what I'd done. He listened to me and when I'd finished, he told me to just correct the damn thing and tried to dismiss me. I kept telling him how I'd made this huge error and really screwed up and he started to yell at me in frustration, which is what I expected."

Dr. Gibson narrowed his eyes into me, leaned over the clinician's counter and spoke confidentially, "Then he stopped yelling at me. He just stopped. He looked me straight in the eyes and said, 'who the hell do you think you are?' I was taken aback. I didn't know what to say. He repeated, 'who the hell do you think you are that you can't make a mistake? Do you think you're God or something? Everybody makes mistakes. Now correct the damn thing and get back to work.' I walked away, corrected the damn mistake and went back to work."

He waited for me to absorb the lesson. He knew I understood. I snapped out of the attentive stupor that his prolonged story had lulled me into, long enough to realize that I'd grown comfortable in his presence. I had become so engrossed in his story that I'd rested two sturdy elbows on the clinician's table to support my weary head.

His smile had faded to a solemn cue for my acknowledgement.

I smiled appreciatively. I got it.

"My father is a perfectionist as well," I admitted.

He nodded. He knew it already.

"Well," I stopped myself for an accuracy check, "he actually only expected it out of the rest of us."

There was a comfortable silence between us as I paused for the realization. Dr. Gibson had helped me rediscover the true motivation for my incessant need for perfection. Some lessons repeat throughout life until you understand them in full.

When I glanced back over to him, he was smiling at me again. "Now go correct the damn paperwork and get back to work. In fact, bring the paperwork to me and I'll help you."

In that moment, I gave in to my spontaneous urge to thank him. "May I hug you?"

He didn't hide his surprise at my reaction. "OF COURSE!" he boomed.

His hug was fatherly and reassuring.

"Thank you," I spoke when we finally spaced our contact. "I needed to hear that story."

I never forgot that day. It tidied up a lot of fear and self-judgment for me. Unencumbered by my disillusioned need for perfection, I discovered for myself my true healing gifts that I always knew I had deep down inside.

There is an old axiom that doctors abide, "Physician Heal Thyself." That wisdom finally awakened in me that day.

Upon my graduation, no instructor was smiling wider than Dr. Hugo Gibson as he reached out, shook my hand and leaned into me one last time.

"Congratulations, Doctor."

A portion of the author's proceeds are donated to educational endeavors.

www.ingramcontent.com/pod-product-compliance
Lightning Source LLC
Chambersburg PA
CBHW072344090426
42741CB00012B/2908